'I have had the joy of knowing Tracy  respect her as a person through who generously.

'The Japanese art of Kintsugi, wh with gold that shines through to enhance the whole piece, is exactly what comes to mind when reading Tracy's account of her personal discovery of the unique love of Father God for each of us, and her invitation for us to discover this love for ourselves.

'Tracy writes so powerfully about the nature of the Father's love for us, revealing his heart in such a beautiful way. Yet perhaps the most powerful parts of this book are those moments when she shares bits of her own story and allows us to glimpse her brokenness, but also to see the enormous grace of God that flows through her as he lovingly restores her to the person he created her to be.'

Revd John Ryeland
Director, The Christian Healing Mission

'Tracy writes about God the Father's kiss with such openness, honesty and sincerity. Based on the assurance of her own relationship with the Triune God, she describes the Father's unconditional love as a 'big' love. She speaks about a generous Father who 'delights' in his children. And a God who longs to be our parent.

'Tracy shares much of her own story, including painful memories and discouragements from the past. In so doing, she is able to empathise with readers who may have struggled to relate to one or other of their earthly parents. But Tracy also confidently shares how she has been able to form a close relationship with her loving heavenly Father – an opportunity open to everyone.

'Tracy has such an amazing gift of being able to hear God speak; and sets us a good example of what it means to really spend time prayerfully listening to him – which is exactly where the book begins: "Some years ago . . . a clear thought came to my heart [when I was praying]: 'Receive the Father's kiss [of love].'"'

Revd Patrick Coghlan
Minister, writer and counsellor

'Above everything else, this book fills me with a deep sense of joy because it's getting to the heart of what we all need to have as our most fundamental foundation: God's unconditional, unchanging and irresistible love. It's giving us insights into learning to live as his beloved, how to rest, relax, and take in to ourselves his most wonderful nurturing presence.

'Over the years I have seen how this love has captured Tracy's heart more and more, changing her into one of the most giving, caring individuals I have ever met, and I recommend this book wholeheartedly to all who want to find this love for themselves.

'Thank you, Tracy, for helping me understand by your life and friendship more about the depth of the Father's love.'

Marilyn Baker
Singer/songwriter and Director, MBM Trust

'All credit to Tracy for sharing so much of herself and her vulnerability in this book. Yet her story, and the journey she has made, her understanding and her wisdom make this book an instrument of hope for all those who cannot understand the concept of a kind, loving heavenly Father. But it does more than give us knowledge, it also leads us gently through a journey of our own experience, giving us time and ideas to allow the Father to minister his love to us, deal with our pain, and allow his grace to inhabit and reveal our true selves. This book has helped me personally, and knowing the amount of need in the church, and the wider world, I shall be recommending it widely.'

Revd Paul Springate
Former Chaplain/Warden, Harnhill Centre of Christian Healing

'Tracy Williamson takes us on a journey of discovery: discovering God's heart. With raw honesty, she shares how God took her from daring to believe she is actually loveable, to daring to receive his love in all its fullness.

'Full of beautifully drawn-together stories, scriptures, and meditations, whether you've ever – or never – realised that God loves you, this book will help you experience his embrace.'

Emily Owen, author

'Although severely deaf, Tracy has an amazing ability to hear the voice of God. Here she shares with us in a profound way a truth God wants each of us to know at the core of our being – that we are unconditionally and eternally loved by the Father. As she explains Bible passages and relates personal stories, Tracy writes with a prophetic edge, bringing a message from God that each of us needs to hear and receive. Tracy embodies powerfully what she writes about, and this makes her words even more special. This is a book to read with an open heart so that you, too, can receive the Father's kiss.'

Tony Horsfall, retreat leader and author

THE
FATHER'S
KISS

LIVING IN THE REALITY
OF GOD'S LOVE

TRACY WILLIAMSON

Authentic

First published 2018 by Authentic Media Limited,
PO Box 6326, Bletchley, Milton Keynes, MK1 9GG.
authenticmedia.co.uk

British Library Cataloguing in Publication Data
A catalogue record for this book is available from the British Library.

ISBN: 978-1-78078-988-0
978-1-78078-989-7 (e-book)

Cover design by
Elisa Pasquadibisceglie
elisapdb7@gmail.com

Printed and bound by CPI Group (UK) Ltd., Croydon, CR0 4YY

Copyright Acknowledgements

Contents

About the Author

Tracy Williamson lives near Tonbridge in Kent, sharing a home with her friend and ministry partner, Marilyn Baker, together with Tracy's hearing dog and Marilyn's guide dog.

Tracy, who became deaf and partially sighted through encephalitis at the age of 2, studied for a BA Hons in English Literature and Education at what is now Hertfordshire University. Tracy became a Christian at the end of her first year whilst going through a time of deep depression, and after graduating, became friends with the blind gospel singer Marilyn Baker. Five months later, Tracy joined Marilyn's ministry, MBM Trust and began sharing her testimony and prophetic words at Marilyn's concerts. Tracy wrote her first book, *The Voice of the Father* (Hodder & Stoughton) in 1995, followed by four shorter books published by New Wine Press between 2004 and 2008.

Today Tracy and Marilyn still travel the country and sometimes abroad taking concerts and church services and also leading rest and renewal days and conferences on experiencing the Father's love, listening to God and being transformed.

For further information about MBM Trust, please visit www.mbm-ministries.org.

If you would like Tracy to come and speak to your church or group about God's Father heart, or for information about the ministry or Tracy's other books, please email: info@mbm-ministries.org.

Confidentiality

Unless permission has been given, people's names have sometimes been changed for the sake of confidentiality.

Acknowledgements

This part is always scary as I am sure I will leave out someone important as there are so many people to thank in bringing this book to birth!

So huge thanks to:

My MBM team and trustees, for all your ongoing support and belief in me.

My lovely prayer supporters, friends and Facebook friends who have stood with me throughout this book's creation. Your prayers have empowered me to keep writing.

Ewa Bem and the unknown lady at the retreat centre who encouraged me.

Jennifer Rees Larcombe, you've given me so much encouragement over the years and once again have written me a wonderful Foreword.

Emily Owen, your friendship and lovely books have inspired me to start writing again myself.

Patrick Coghlan, you've always taken a keen interest in my writing and offered wise advice and encouragement.

Peter Smart, you unknowingly answered my prayer for confirmation about the theme.

David Cook, you diligently checked the manuscript as I wrote it – a much needed help with my tendency to typos!

Thanks to all who have contributed so much to the book's richness by contributing your stories or experiences of God's love – Lynn, Wendy, Lilian, Fiona, Teresa, Sharon, Heidi and numerous others whose stories have inspired me or whose comments about their own dads have given me much food for thought.

Marilyn, your loving relationship with God has opened my eyes and heart to his love, and your amazing friendship and patience have helped me so much.

Rachel, for all your practical help and support.

Thanks Lilian, Eve, Marilyn, Mum and other close friends and family, you've all patiently tolerated me ignoring everything but the computer screen for weeks at a time!

Thanks Donna, Becky, Sheila and the Authentic team, you encouraged me from the very beginning.

Thanks to the many authors and speakers who have given me deep inspiration and understanding of God's Father heart.

And my deep thanks to all those who over the years have had such a healing impact on my life and enabled me to truly enter into a Father-daughter relationship with God. Without your input, prayers and love, this book could never have been written.

Finally, the most heartfelt thanks to God my heavenly Father and his amazing love in making us all his beloved children and heirs.

Tracy Williamson

I dedicate this book to John and Amanda Duncan, for the wonderful way you showed me the Father's love when I was in such need.

And to all those who have known the pain of fatherlessness –
May you discover the joy of being God's beloved child.

Foreword

In my work in prayer ministry and counselling I see so many people who are carrying deep pain resulting from inadequate or destructive fathering. We tend to think first of sexual abuse in this context, but lasting scars can also be caused by indifferent, absent, distant, critical or angry fathers. They may love their children but simply do not know how to show it. It is also a tragic truth that, whether we know it or not, our understanding of the Fatherhood of God is formed in part from our experience of our own fathers. So many people I see think of Father God as a cross between a headmaster and a bank manager! Even Philip, who lived with Jesus, beseeched him, 'Lord, show us the Father and we will be satisfied' (John 14:8 NLT). Perhaps he could not equate the gentle, accepting, constant love of Jesus with his own father?

I have known and loved Tracy Williamson as a friend for many years now. As I read her story it was hard to believe that someone with such a difficult childhood could possibly have 'turned' into such a beautiful, loving and gracious adult. Counselling textbooks would have predicted someone so very different! She suffered such destructive fathering and yet this book tells the story of her journey into healing through learning the truth of God as a Father who loves, approves and delights in his child.

Each of the sections in the book features one of the attributes of the Fatherhood of God and it was so helpful to me, as I worked through, to have the breaks in the text for reflection and prayer. One of the most powerful concepts for me was gaining a new and deeper appreciation of the meaning of the Father's kiss.

This is not always an easy story to read, because journeys into healing seldom are, but it is so worthwhile.

I do believe there is a part of us that always yearns for the fathering we so badly need – this book was so beneficial in helping to 'show me the Father'.

Jennifer Rees Larcombe
Director, Beauty from Ashes

Introduction

Some years ago, while on a retreat, a clear thought came to my heart: 'Receive the Father's kiss.' I didn't understand what it meant or if it was even biblical. I had been praying about writing my testimony, but as much as I tried, nothing happened. Was I pushing at a door that wasn't meant to open? I had written a series of short books a few years before, but then a life disappointment had made me lose confidence. Would I ever write again?

The next day, my retreat director, Ewa, assigned me a passage from Luke which I was amazed to discover was the story of the prodigal son. This had been a great source of help to me in my early Christian life and I also use it in the conferences I lead with Marilyn Baker. I read it slowly, trying to be open to what God might show me. Suddenly a phrase jumped out at me: 'He ran to his son, threw his arms round him and kissed him' (Luke 15:20).

'Kissed him' – I had never taken those words in before. I'd been wondering if the idea about receiving the Father's kiss was scriptural, and here it was, in one of my favourite Bible stories.

'Lord, what are you telling me?'

As I sat before him, the idea began to crystallise, that he wanted me to write about his great affection and unconditional love towards all his children; so that all could begin to experience his affection for themselves.

I felt daunted. 'Lord, how can I do that? I haven't written for years,' I protested. I prayed he would confirm this word and take my fear away about starting to write again. The next morning when I went into breakfast, a lady glanced up and then stared at me with surprised recognition. A short while later she came over with a note – she'd obviously known that I couldn't hear, and as this was a silent retreat she couldn't chat anyway. When I read the note I was overwhelmed. She'd read my book *Encountering God*, and loved it. I'd mentioned this retreat centre so she'd decided to come and had brought my book to be her retreat reading material. I felt humbled, but when I came to the last phrase I was completely gobsmacked. 'Your book has brought me so much closer to God,' she wrote. 'Whatever you do, keep writing.'

Well, it couldn't be much clearer confirmation, but what about the theme? Could I have really heard God correctly to write about the Father's kiss?

After returning home I went to my church in Tonbridge. It usually opens with a long time of worship and we were all ready, when Pete, the pastor, came to the microphone: 'Before we worship,' he said, 'I believe God is saying something very important. He loves us and wants to kiss us with his affection. He wants us to understand what his kiss of love is and how you can experience in your heart that he loves you . . . '

Pete continued, but once again I was full of wonder. I'd asked God for confirmation and he was giving it, over and over.

That all happened in 2013 and it has taken me until now to bring this book to completion. It has been quite tough as the theme is one I've needed to take on board and experience deeply for myself. It has brought up deep pain, yet taken me to the heights of thankfulness in understanding his amazing love afresh.

He has wonderfully guided me in its composition too. When I was on retreat again later on and walking in the lovely grounds, I noticed that all the pathways ultimately led back to the centre. He showed me this was a picture of how to write the book – to include all the little pathways by which people might grow in their understanding of his love: Bible teaching, poems, stories, reflections, prophetic words, humour and poignancy. I was amazed at how clearly he was leading me.

I have tried to follow his loving direction, and the result is this book. The chapters progress through helping us to understand his love and build it as a foundation into our lives, to discovering ways we can grow in our relationship with him and realise we can be a channel of his love to others. It is an interactive book with 'Pause and reflect' moments interspersed throughout each chapter. I really recommend that you do take that time to reflect and write your responses down in a journal. They may well become treasures of his love to you in days to come.

It's my prayer that as you read you will laugh, cry, be drawn into the Father's love and anointed to give it away.

Tracy Williamson 2017

Prologue

The Father I Never Knew

As I grew up I looked for a dad
With whom I could be me.
A dad who would relish me being his child
Who would cuddle me on his knee.
A dad who through being in my life
Would heal my fear of the unknown,
Would still my cries and hush my demands
With a love both spoken and shown.

I looked for a dad who would make me laugh
And see life through the eyes of hope.
A dad who would draw out the best in me
And help me to reach my full scope.
I looked for a dad who would be gently strong
And would lovingly guide my ways;
A dad whose touch would be nurture and life
As I walked through life's every phase.

I looked for a dad who with pure respect
Would see the woman I was created to be;
And through his gentle kiss of fatherly love
Would protect yet set me free.

This is what I hoped but like so many
The reality was rather stark.
For the father experiences I had, stole
My innocence and left a deep mark.
A father would help me realise my dreams

And discover the gifts deep within;
But my dreams were shattered with mocking words
And my gifts trampled then thrown in the bin.

But at that place where trust had died
I discovered a love tender and true;
It sought me out and would not let go
And a flame of hope kindled and grew.
This love flowed from my true Father's heart
Who chose me and called me by name;
He formed me in my mother's womb,
And danced with joy when I came.

He reached out to me with words of love
And his tenderness melted my heart;
He said he'd given his Son for me,
That we need never again, be apart.
I cried and I could not take his love,
So full of shame and anger and fear;
He listened and wept, as I shared things unsaid
And I never felt compassion so dear.

I suddenly knew that with all he'd been through
He truly had carried my pain;
His blood flowed for me, as he hung on that tree,
All my sin, my loss, my shame.
With tears I opened my heart to him
And I will never again be alone;
He heals my fears and stills my cries
With a love both spoken and shown.

I now have a dad who makes me laugh
And see life through the eyes of hope;
A dad who draws out the best in me,
And helps me to reach my full scope.

I now have a dad who is supremely strong
Who lovingly guides my ways;
A dad whose touch is nurture and life
Healing wounds from my earliest days.

I now have a dad who with pure respect
Sees the woman I was created to be
And through his affirming kiss of love
Opens the fullness of life to me.

Tracy Williamson 2014

1

What is the Father's Kiss?

All I want to do is to bless you. All I want to do is pour out my love. To show you how dear you are to me. For me there is no other. To me you are a pearl of great price.

Marilyn Baker

Extract taken from the song 'The Father's Song of Love' by Marilyn Baker. Copyright © 1998 Marilyn Baker Music.*

Father's call of love

As a single, childless woman, it may seem strange that I am embarking on another book about God's Father heart. What can I add that's different? My early experiences were full of the pain of serious illness causing undiagnosed deafness, compounded by deep loss when my dad died of cancer when I was 7. The man who replaced him was abusive and was thus never Dad to me. Indeed, his treatment nearly led to me ending my life before I'd stepped fully into adulthood. So how can I claim to know God's love in such a way that I think I can help others to find him? How can I describe a God who is caring, affectionate, affirming and trusting towards us, when I have little human experience of such love, either giving or receiving it?

One day when I was battling with this, the Holy Spirit spoke into my heart: 'If only you knew how much my heart breaks for all my children who don't know a father's love and daren't believe that I could love them. I long for them to know how dear they are to me, that there's nothing I wouldn't do for them. My love overrides the deepest rejections, failures and brokenness. I want all my children to know me as Father and that they *can* experience my love.'

These words awoke a real desire to know him that way myself, but would this be possible for me and the many others who find it so hard to trust in his love?

'Father, I feel there's such a barrier in my heart,' I prayed; and as I sat quietly, a deeper sense of his response came to me.

'You've been broken and still have scars. There are still times when you hate yourself and think I will punish you. But despite that you still seek to know me; you've opened your heart to my voice and heard me speaking to you. You've known my provision and care. You are learning to trust me and set new foundations in your life which bring you into wholeness. Because of this you truly are equipped to share your message that others too may dare to believe I love them unconditionally. Never look at what you perceive to be your lack. Rather, look to me and what I am doing in your life.'

This word filled me with hope. God wants us to believe that he loves us as a good father loves his children. Many of us have lacked love and nurture from someone who cares about us unconditionally. If you haven't experienced love like this, the message of this book is that it is not too late; you can still find it in your heavenly Father. He is constantly acting on your behalf that you may know how beloved you are to him, and see the enemy's negative strongholds in your life destroyed.

Jesus defeated Satan that we might know the truth of God's love

To become someone who lives as God's beloved child requires a willingness to do battle against the enemy. We are at war, and Satan uses every means possible to imprison us, but he is already defeated through the cross. Satan specialises in whispering lies into our hearts, but God frees us as we trust in his love and truth. He cares about every detail of our lives and is always rooting for us, whatever our circumstances. Peter teaches us about this battle in 1 Peter 5:7–9:

> Cast all your anxiety on him because he cares for you. Be alert and of sober mind. Your enemy the devil prowls around like a roaring lion looking for someone to devour. Resist him, standing firm in the faith.

'Cast all your anxiety on him'... '*all* your anxiety'. That doesn't mean only your concern for loved ones or world crises, it also means the inner fears, rejections and guilt which cripple you. I've often felt paralysed by fear or self-rejection, but Peter tells us to cast (i.e. to hurl) all those negative things upon Jesus. Why? Because in Peter's words again: 'He cares for you'. He cares for you. He loves you. You are the apple of his eye (see Ps. 17:8). He weeps with your tears and shares your every joy.

Peter said we have to 'resist [the devil], standing firm in the faith'. To resist means to push with all our weight against something that is opposing us. If we don't believe the truth of what God says about us, we won't have any weight to resist with. Even our churches can make us view ourselves negatively. The other day an acquaintance of Marilyn's popped round and whilst they were chatting she said, 'I'm so sick of hearing that I'm a miserable sinner.' Her church's teaching was crushing her, rather than lifting her up into peace and joy. She was hungry for the life-giving truth of God's unconditional love. Are you hungry too? I know I am.

From despair to hope

It has been an ongoing journey for me to really learn to live as God's beloved daughter and I'm still on that journey now. It began when I was 18 and my self-esteem was extremely low after years of rejection and abuse. I was at teacher training college, but was finding it a huge struggle with my deafness and insecurity. I felt I had no natural authority to control the children, and even though I was studying for a degree, I felt paralysed by my fears. I shared lodgings with another first-year student who was kind and extrovert, but I hardly said a word to her. I could be surrounded by a crowd of friendly students and feel totally alone. Every night I cried myself to sleep, weeping as silently as I could so as not to wake Helen. Although I knew she was a Christian, and through her I had met other Christian students who had become my circle too, it never occurred to me to try to talk to anyone about my struggles. How could anyone else help?

One night I felt so low that I tried to commit suicide. I wandered away from my lodgings in a daze, only conscious of the heaviness within my heart. It was like a rock-hard weight, nothing could shift it. Without noting where I was going, I suddenly found myself standing by a small lake on the local common. It was raining and cold. No one else was around and I stood staring at the glistening water. I felt what a relief it would be to sink beneath the surface and not have to struggle any more. No one would miss me, I thought. After all, I was nothing, just an empty shell, a useless lump of cells thrown together to form a travesty of a person.

Deep down I knew this was wrong thinking and that I would be missed. I knew my family loved me, even though they'd caused me pain. Yet despite this, the bleakness of my despair was stronger. I felt I would always be stuck in the shame and fear of my past. Staring at the water, I felt mesmerised, as if it was calling me to come and enter its peace. I put my bag down and walked forward to the very edge. There was no drop down to the water, I could just step straight into it, but I knew from a previous attempt to paddle that the bottom soon dropped away and the lake became deep. It was cold too which would probably immobilise me, and as a very weak swimmer, it wouldn't take long to drown.

I stood shivering as these thoughts went through my head. It was raining hard now and the wind was growing stronger. I felt totally alone. I took a step forward and my feet sank into the mud. I took another and almost fell as it closed round my shoes, sucking my feet downwards. 'I'll ruin my shoes,' I thought, and almost smiled at the incongruity of my thoughts. After all, what did it matter?

Shivering with cold and fear, I took another step and the freezing water lapped round my ankles. I knew that just a little further the ground would shelve down steeply: if I kept going, all this torment would soon be over. I heard that voice whispering in my head as it had been increasingly these last weeks. 'Go on, Tracy, end it all. You'll never be anything but a disappointment. You're just a lazy good-for-nothing. No one will ever love you. You'll never do anything of any worth. You're useless, stupid, ugly . . . '

I wept as I edged further in. I'd hardly ever let myself cry, certainly not at home, as it gave my stepfather too much power over me. I'd spent years pushing down my reactions to the bullying at school, and the shame and fear that were my constant companions at home. Now, in the silence of this cold March night, the pain of those buried feelings overwhelmed me.

The water was now just above my ankles and I could feel the ground starting to fall away. I knew that soon it would get so much deeper that I wouldn't be able to stay upright. I would fall, I would not struggle and that would be the end.

Shivering violently, I paused for a final moment. If I had any hope of changing to become the kind of person I longed to be, I would not go through with this. But I'd gone to college full of dreams that I would be the centre of a crowd of friends, having fun, even making people laugh. I'd seen myself having an impact on the children I would be teaching, someone they would come to with their problems. I'd longed to have this kind of teacher myself and I did have one who was very caring when I reached the sixth form, but by then I was too rooted in the pattern of hiding to be able to open up properly to her.

I knew now that I could not be what my dreams had given me such false hope about. I was still a loser and always would be. Discovering that I was unable to effectively teach had been the last straw, the confirmation that everything that had been said and done to me was valid.

I turned my head for a final moment and gazed in the direction of the road back to my lodgings. 'Goodbye,' I whispered, and lifted my foot to step forward.

But in that instant I knew I would not do it. It wasn't that my despair lessened, or even my desire to die. It wasn't that I was too scared, as I was more scared of trying to continue living. No one disturbed me and there was no obvious spiritual encounter that stopped me. But as I lifted my foot and was already beginning to fall, I just knew it wasn't going to happen. I did end up fully in the water but only in the process of turning around and scrambling back to the path. My heart was dead and cold like a stone. I emptied my shoes of water, picked up my bag and crept home.

Father God was watching over me

I didn't tell anyone what I had so nearly done, so I was shocked a week later when another student invited me into her room and, over coffee, told me that she was a Christian and that, while praying, God had put an urgency within her to tell me that he loved me and wanted me to know him as Father. I was stunned as she spoke about the miracle of his love. I had never thought much about God but now Ruth was saying that he not only existed but knew my name and had communicated with her about me and given her a glimpse into my deepest pain. I can still remember the quietness of that room, sitting on floor cushions as Ruth talked. My arms clasped around my knees, long, permed 'poodle' hairstyle and big glasses hiding my face. Although I found it hard to hear in a crowd, one-to-one was often fine at that time, so I didn't have much difficulty in following Ruth. As she spoke about God's love and desire for us to know him, I found something loosening deep inside of me. Occasionally I glanced up and was drawn by the certainty shining from her eyes. This wasn't just something she had studied like our subjects at college, this was someone she knew and whose love she was convinced of. How could that be? How could you be so sure of something invisible and unverifiable that you would glow with the strength of your feelings just as if you'd met someone and discovered they were also attracted to you? I didn't understand and yet I felt myself pulled in by Ruth's joyful certainty. The peace in the room wrapped around me and the tiniest crack opened in my heart. Maybe there was hope, even for someone like me? Maybe death wasn't the only answer after all?

God's heart of love

That night, and in fact through that whole sequence of events, I was beginning to glimpse the fact that God loved me and was seeking me out even when I didn't know if I believed in his existence. I think what happened in the lake when I retraced my steps just in time, and then in

Ruth's room, was something like what happened to the young man in the story Jesus told in Luke 15:11–24 whom we know as the prodigal son.

Jesus continued: 'There was a man who had two sons. The younger one said to his father, "Father, give me my share of the estate." So he divided his property between them. Not long after that, the younger son got together all he had, set off for a distant country and there squandered his wealth in wild living. After he had spent everything, there was a severe famine in that whole country, and he began to be in need. So he went and hired himself out to a citizen of that country, who sent him to his fields to feed pigs. He longed to fill his stomach with the pods that the pigs were eating, but no one gave him anything.

When he came to his senses, he said . . . "I will set out and go back to my father and say to him: Father, I have sinned against heaven and against you. I am no longer worthy to be called your son; make me like one of your hired servants." So he got up and went to his father.

But while he was still a long way off, his father saw him and was filled with compassion for him; he ran to his son, threw his arms round him and kissed him.

The son said to him, "Father, I have sinned against heaven and against you. I am no longer worthy to be called your son."

But the father said to his servants, "Quick! Bring the best robe and put it on him. Put a ring on his finger and sandals on his feet. Bring the fattened calf and kill it. Let's have a feast and celebrate. For this son of mine was dead and is alive again; he was lost and is found." So they began to celebrate.'

Do you find it hard to imagine God having such strong emotions? Jesus told this story specifically to reveal the depth of his Father's love. It was a picture of how God never gives up loving us. The son had made a terrible choice, virtually wishing his father dead by demanding his inheritance and then disappearing without trace. In modern terms it would be as if he had thrown away his mobile phone, shut down his email and Facebook accounts, changed address and gone ex-directory. He didn't want to be found. He wanted nothing more to do with his father.

The pain of losing a child, for whatever reason, is beyond all other pains. There is something raw and primal that cries out when a loved child goes missing or is in pain. It causes otherwise rational parents to act totally out of character. We see this same desperate longing in the father's response. He pushes aside all his usual priorities so he can focus on his son. His heart aches as he stares across the desert, day by day, year by year. One day a black dot suddenly appears, so far away that the father wonders if he's imagined it. That had happened before, the conviction rising that his son was approaching and would soon be home. Each time, he'd raced outside, shouting his son's name. Last time the servants had been openly mocking and his elder son had forbidden him to disgrace the family like that again.

But this time the black dot was real. This was no trick of his eyes. This was truly his son. The father ran, uncaring of what people thought or of the undignified picture he presented. All he wanted was to embrace his lost son and welcome him home.

Jesus knew his Father

Do you know that God loves you in that same impassioned way? Jesus' listeners thought of God as Lord and Judge, but Jesus knew him, and wanted us to know him, as Father. Jesus saw his Father constantly watching over his children, even those who wanted nothing to do with him. We cannot do anything to make him love us, for he already does. He has loved us from the beginning of time and even when we ignore him, he still does, always longing for us to enter the joy of being his beloved children.

As we read in John 1:11–13:

> He came to that which was his own, but his own did not receive him. Yet to all who did receive him, to those who believed in his name, he gave the right to become children of God – children born not of natural descent, nor of human decision or a husband's will, but born of God.

We rejected him and still do; even as Christians we reject him and refuse to let him into certain areas of our lives. We want him on our terms, not on his, and like that younger son, we go off and do our own thing. Or we demand our rights from our Father without ever taking the time to see what he is really like. We waste the kingdom resources that he gives us so freely, yet starve ourselves of his love. We choose to relate to him as servants rather than as beloved sons and daughters, but still he never stops loving and watching over us and calling us to come and be with him.

God loves you

The heart of this message is that you matter to your heavenly Father. His love is real and lasting. You cannot ever disappoint him, for he knows and understands you through and through. He knows the things that thrill your heart and motivate you. He knows what comforts and excites you. He knows what makes you laugh or cry. He also knows those weaker inner areas of your soul that act like a kind of quicksand and draw you to do things you hate doing but which you feel helpless to change. He sees each act, each thought, each sin. He may hate the act, hate the thought and hate the sin, but he loves you. And his love can radically change you from the inside out.

You cannot love someone you don't know. You may think you love a celebrity, but you're really drawn to the external things like their glamour, sex appeal or success. But you don't actually *know* them. Are they kind, patient, exciting, flamboyant or introspective? Are they readers, sports-mad, fashion icons, church leaders or night-clubbers? Are they hot-tempered, unfeeling, loving or shy? You may get tiny glimpses through social media and news articles, but it will still only be a controlled glimpse. You can only grow to love someone when you spend time in their company, notice their habits and discover the things that make them tick.

So when Father God says he loves you, he also means that he knows you. He takes joy in seeing how you live out all that he has created you to be. He does not look upon you from afar and say, 'I love the idea of knowing that man or woman.' Rather, he says: 'I watch over you while you sleep. I am with you when you wake. Every moment I am alongside you. Nothing about you is hidden to me. Even the obscurest workings of the tiniest cells of your body are all known to me.'

Some of us may find the concept of such knowledge scary, like Big Brother's watching you. Am I a puppet on a string? Do I have any real autonomy if he already knows everything about me?

But, as we read in 1 John 4:18:

> There is no fear in love. But perfect love drives out fear, because fear has to do with punishment. The one who fears is not made perfect in love.

God's love is the perfect love that drives fear away, not that produces it. His knowledge springs from a heart of love, not from any desire to control us. We can be secure in his love, knowing that he is with us and is totally for us.

Listen to these amazing verses from Psalm 139:1–4:

> O Lord, you have examined my heart and know everything about me. You know when I sit down or stand up. You know my thoughts even when I'm far away. You see me when I travel and when I rest at home. You know everything I do. You know what I am going to say even before I say it, Lord (NLT).

The most important thing

Are you beginning to get a glimpse of just how big God's love is for you? Whatever you are doing, whether it feels mundane or important, is significant to him. He thinks about you and knows what you are going to say, even before you know yourself. He longs for you to know the joy of being loved in this way. The intimacy of his love must never just be words, but deeply experienced in our everyday lives.

This is hard for us to believe, but there is nothing more important; it's even more important than making good relationships, having children, caring for our dependants or ensuring our future is secure . . .

There are millions more life goals, just as many as there are people, for we are all unique and have different things that drive us. Yet the greatest need for us all is to know we are unconditionally loved by God. Knowing his love and loving him in return creates a foundation of peace and power in our lives that cannot be replicated by anything else. It has released me from the hopelessness of feeling I was doomed to fail in life, to living with a whole new joy and purpose.

The furious longing of God

The following is a true story showing the transforming power of a father's love which deeply touched my heart. It is from a book by Brennan Manning called *The Furious Longing of God*. The story is set in the 1960s when Brennan was teaching at a university in Ohio. He tells of an agnostic student called Larry who was very messed up. He was short and obese with terrible personal hygiene, acne and a lisp. He had no friends and was in no clubs. Brennan says: 'In all my days I have never met anybody with such low self-esteem. He told me that when he looked in the mirror each morning, he spit at it.'

At Christmas Larry went home to be with his father, who was extremely refined and found it hard to engage with his son. When Larry returned to university, his father decided to travel with him part way. As they got off the bus they saw a group of men nearby. In Brennan's words:

They began making loud and degrading remarks like 'Oink, oink, look at that fat pig . . . if that pig was my kid, I'd hide him in the basement, I'd be so embarrassed.' Another said, 'I wouldn't. If that slob was my kid, he'd be out the door so fast, he wouldn't know if he's on foot or horseback. Hey, pig! Give us your best oink!' . . .

Larry Malaney told me that in that moment . . . his father reached out and embraced him, kissed him on the lips, and said: 'Larry, if your mother and I live to be two hundred years old, that wouldn't be long enough to thank God for the gift He gave to us in you. I am so proud that you're my son!'

Brennan goes on to describe the amazing transformation this act of fatherly love had upon Larry. He began to change both inwardly and outwardly, transforming himself to such an extent that he started dating a girl and became president of one of the fraternities. He excelled in his degree and started going to Brennan's office to ask questions about faith. In 1974 he was ordained a priest. To quote:

> for the last twenty years, he's been a missionary in South America, a man totally sold out to Jesus Christ. Do you know why? . . . it was because of a day, long ago, standing at a bus stop, when his . . . father healed him . . . His father looked deeply into his son's eyes, saw the good in Larry Malaney that Larry couldn't see for himself, affirmed him with a furious love, and changed the whole direction of his son's life.[1]

'Changed the whole direction of his son's life.' This truth still grips my heart. It's not just that it's a nice story about a father's change of heart towards his son; it's not just that it's moving or even that it's challenging. What grips me is the life-transforming power in that father's act of love. Love never operates in a vacuum: a sweet action or word fading away into oblivion. True love bears fruit, in this case the fruit of a healed heart and the motivation to live differently. As I read it again, especially the words:

> His father looked deeply into his son's eyes, saw the good in Larry Malaney that Larry couldn't see for himself, affirmed him with a furious love, and changed the whole direction . . .

I felt chills going up and down my spine. I sensed the Spirit of God speaking into my heart: 'So many of my children are living as orphans and don't know what it means to be loved. All they see are the flaws that others never fail to point out to them. They hate themselves and are blind to the beauty that I have written into their lives. But I am there. I love them. I look in their eyes and see the reflection of my precious Son. I long to embrace and kiss them with my love and affirmation; to tell them the truth, that I love them with a love that cries out, "I am proud to be your Father."'

As these words filled my spirit, I sensed his longing for us to receive this passionate love, even if we've never known it humanly. As we read the Bible he will open it up and meet us in the words. We may experience a physical touch of his love, or hear him speaking into our fears as we pray. He may come to us through the comfort and help of others; or through music, creation, or children . . .

The key is he will. He will, because he loves us and the desire of his heart is always that we know his love in all its depth and reality. As we go further into this book, we will explore some of those ways he shows himself to us. We'll also look at some of the things that make us hold back, and we'll learn to let them go and start to take steps deeper into his love.

 Pause and reflect

- How does the phrase 'the Father loves you' make you feel?
- Are you aware of hurts in your life that rob you of a childlike trust?
- Spend time quietly praying to entrust those hurts to him and ask him to help you discover what it means to be loved.
- Thinking of these three stories: my own, the prodigal son and Larry's story, what do they show you about God's love for you?
- Looking back in your life, is there a time when you have struggled with a deep sense of hopelessness?
- Holding that memory up before the Lord, ask the Holy Spirit to reveal how the Father was reaching out to help you in that situation. Don't analyse if your thoughts are authentic; just accept that he is communicating to you.
- Thank him for any new insight or understanding, and ask him to show you how to live in the truth of it.
- Thank him for his tender care and everlasting commitment to you.

2

A Father to the Fatherless

A father of the fatherless and a judge and protector of the widows is God in His holy habitation. God places the solitary in families and gives the desolate a home in which to dwell; He leads the prisoners out to prosperity; but the rebellious dwell in a parched land.

Psalm 68:5,6 (AMPC)

A dad who is there for his children

Once I was on holiday abroad and my friends and I were waiting for a bus. It was late and while everyone was impatiently hanging around, I suddenly noticed a couple with their two small sons. The dad was playing with the children, encouraging them to race up and down a short slope and see how far they could jump. Every now and again he scooped them up and tickled them until they were helpless with laughter, then let them retaliate by launching themselves at him, using their heads as battering rams, which must have been quite painful. At one point the youngest, maybe about 3, came running down the slope and in his excitement lost control, but Dad was there immediately and lifted him up, wrapping his protective arms around him, and the little boy's scream of fear instantly turned to happy giggles as his dad smothered him with 'monster' kisses.

I found myself caught up in this joyful yet protective play. It was so clear that the dad really loved them and was watching over their every move, delighting in their fun. I am more used, even in this day, to the mums being the hands-on ones, but this mum seemed hardly engaged, whilst the dad was fully there for them. It made me feel happy yet sad too as I realised I had never enjoyed that kind of bonding and fun with my own dad. There was an ache inside of me, a lack that I had no idea how to satisfy.

So many are in that same position and, like me, feel heart hunger for what they have never had. It was beautiful to see this dad so close to his children, yet it was bittersweet, full of pain too.

'Father, I don't know what it means to be fathered,' I whispered. 'How can I ever enter into that carefree belovedness, when it's just never been part of my life?'

As I stood quietly, I felt a peace enter my heart. And then words from Psalm 68 came to my mind: 'A father to the fatherless . . . ' As I thought about those words and the other beautiful expressions of God's love and care that the psalm depicts, I began to understand that God is not restrained by either our positive or negative experiences, but he longs for us to know what it means to be fathered in the wonderful way that only he can. His name and therefore his character is 'father to the fatherless'. He is Father to all, but especially to everyone who has not experienced being fathered in life.

We are all made in his image and even though we are flawed, we know that we should provide for our children, nurture, affirm and care for them. All of this comes from him. He is the ultimate provider, nurturer, carer and comforter. When he affirms us, his words are true and life-giving, never the false flattery we often give each other. His love is ready for us to take hold of at every moment. He can truly heal the wounds of rejection and lack that so many of us experience.

How may that come about?

Simon

On one occasion I was helping at a local Alpha course. It was the Holy Spirit weekend and while we were all praying for the Holy Spirit to move amongst us, I saw a vision of a young boy playing ball in his garden. No one was with him so he was aimlessly throwing the ball back and forth against the wall. He looked very lonely. Then the picture changed and

I saw a tall man stand next to the boy and rest his arm over his shoulder. He took the ball and soon they were both throwing it for the other to catch. There was now a sense of fun and companionship that was totally missing before. I knew that God wanted to show someone that he understood their pain. After I shared the vision, a young man leapt up.

'How do you know about my life? Who's talked to you about me?' he blurted out.

I was shocked at the immediate response and it was obvious the young man was in great emotional distress.

'It's your heavenly Father,' I replied. 'He has shown me this because he wants to help you.'

'How does he know?' he cried. 'I used to stand out there week after week playing ball on my own. I longed for Dad to play with me but he was never home. If he did come home he looked through me as if I was invisible. And then he left when I was 12. It was my fault. I must have been bad and driven him away.'

By now I was in tears too and so were several others in the group. I sensed the Father's tender desire to heal this man's deep wound of abandonment. How could I help him to find hope when his trust had been so broken by his earthly dad?

'So you remember playing ball on your own like that?' I asked.

He nodded.

'Well,' I said hesitantly. 'I believe God is telling you that he was with you and felt your pain and he wants to show you that he is the Father that will always be there for you. He was there then and he is here now too, and he loves you as his son. I believe he is saying, "You must not blame yourself. It was your father's weakness that caused him to reject you, it wasn't you."' I took his hand. 'Anything you've done in your life that hasn't been good, he forgives you, if only you will receive that. You don't have to understand everything; you just need to accept his love.'

There was stillness in the room and I could tell he was listening. The vicar encouraged him to respond and others in the group also lovingly shared how God had healed their own hurts. Later we were all in tears again when Simon prayed, thanking Jesus for dying for him and asking him to come into his life and to show him the Father's love.

The Father's kiss

What happened that afternoon was an example of the Father's kiss of love. Just as the father in the prodigal son story had been constantly watching out for his lost son, longing to restore him to sonship, so God had been there throughout Simon's childhood and was now giving him a 'kiss' of loving restoration through that prophetic vision. Simon knew that only God could have given that picture and it convinced him that he was real and cared about him. As a result he became a Christian.

The touch of God's love upon our hearts is powerful and effective to start us on the path to a transformed life. In this case the kiss came through a vision from the Holy Spirit, but there are myriads of ways through which God works, and we'll be exploring more of them throughout the book.

 Pause and reflect

- Looking back at Psalm 68:5, how do you react to this description of God as 'father to the fatherless'?
- Would you say that like Simon, you have experienced a lack of fathering in your life? How does that make you feel inside?
- The vision showed that God had been there throughout those lonely years of Simon's life. What does that say to you as you reflect on your own life?
- If you have painful memories of rejection, lift them up to your heavenly Father, who sees and understands. Ask him to enable you to see his loving presence in those memories.
- Spend a few moments reflecting on any scriptures, insights or pictures that come to you. Thank him that he is truly your Father and always will be.

The Father's kindness

When someone plants a little kiss on their child's head it shows their tender desire to protect and love him or her. They are developing the bond of affection and it's beautiful to see the baby babbling happily as he gazes back at them. Such actions are familiar to us, but have we ever realised that they are a reflection of God's fatherly affection and kindness towards us, as expressed in these lovely verses from Hosea 11:1–4?

> When Israel was a child, I loved him, and out of Egypt I called my son . . . It was I who taught Ephraim to walk, taking them by the arms; but they did not realise it was I who healed them. I led them with cords of human kindness, with ties of love. To them I was like one who lifts a little child to the cheek, and I bent down to feed them.

God spoke these words prophetically through Hosea to his people, Israel, whom he loved as a parent loves their child. The Israelites were rebellious, following the evil ways of the tribes around them. They had forsaken God but still he wanted them to know how tenderly he loved them, and all of us. He carries us and takes us by the hands to teach us to walk. He lifts us up to his cheek for a kiss, and feeds us. This is beautiful 'motherly' language using images all of us can identify with. But how do we actually equate these images with God when we can neither see nor touch him?

One thing that strikes me is the phrase 'with cords of human kindness'. The phrase 'human kindness' shows us that God chooses to make himself known through ways we can understand. So he provides for our needs, comforts us when we are sad, and affirms and guides us. These are his kisses of kindness and he uses people to show them to us. I will continue my story now, sharing how he touched my own heart through beautiful acts of kindness when I was in great need.

My story continued

In chapter 1, I shared how God met with me through Ruth, when I was in a very dark place. Shortly after that conversation I began talking to other Christian students and reading some of the Bible. I was filled with hope when Ruth shared that God had told her to speak to me about his Father love. It was too specific to just dismiss. However, I was still struggling with my past, and the years of pain couldn't be annihilated just like that.

One day I was reading a little pamphlet Ruth had given me called *Journey into Life* (Falcon Books) and suddenly felt I must talk to God myself and not just listen to other people's experiences. I needed to open my own heart up to him.

The final page listed the steps to faith with a suggested prayer. It was a typical sinner's prayer, although at that time I had no idea what that was. I read it slowly, trying to understand what it meant. Then, for the first time ever, I started to pray. I was using the set prayer, but I soon found myself talking to him from my heart. I said that I wanted to know him like Ruth did and that I was beginning to understand that he'd died for me because he loved me. I was crying out, wanting to feel his love inside me. It was muddled but I meant it, and for the first time I deliberately reached beyond myself in the hope of being changed.

I often share my testimony in Marilyn's concerts, and I always recall my amazement that God became real to me in that moment despite me not being able to see or touch him. I was like a hard shell inside, and yet I suddenly knew that he was there and that he loved me.

That was the beginning of my Christian journey. I was excited and hopeful as the Christians at college drew me into their midst and gave me the sense of belonging I'd longed for. I started going to church, praying and acting like all the others. Outwardly all was well, but inwardly I still battled with overwhelmingly negative feelings, as if I was an empty void. Nothing seemed powerful enough to change that, not even God, despite all my hopes. One day another student made a mildly negative remark and it was the trigger that blew away the walls I'd carefully constructed for the wounded me to hide behind. An explosion of buried raw emotions surged through me and I felt everyone despised me as much as I despised myself. I looked around the dining hall where we were having our evening meal. Everyone except me was talking and laughing. I would never be able to be part of a group or to hold my own socially. I was a misfit and God had done nothing to change me. It had been pointless believing in him. Shaking with anger, I violently pushed away my tray and, ignoring the startled exclamation from the student next to me, jumped up and ran from the room. I couldn't stay in this place that had led me to falsely believe there was hope. I needed to get away.

In my turmoil I didn't even go back to my hall to pack. I was determined I was leaving forever, but I ran from the campus without any plan. I had my bag of college files and a small-change purse. My clothes, money and bank cards were all left behind. I walked blindly, only aware of the great pain in my heart. I didn't care what others thought. I just needed to get as far away as possible. 'You deceived me, God!' I shouted, as I ran down a country road in the pouring rain. 'You're no more powerful than anything else. Nothing can change me.' Tears ran down my face as I remembered the pain of my stepfather's abuse, my terror of his touch and his manic rages. He was the powerful one who could do whatever he wanted, and even my own dad had seemed distant. The pain was overwhelming and I ran all the faster trying to escape it.

Eventually I was exhausted and soaked through from the constant rain. It was thundering, and lightning streaked the sky. A dark shape loomed up in front of me and I realised it was a bus shelter. I collapsed on the seat, shaking, buffeted by the uproar of wind and pain.

The words came with a startling clarity: 'I love you and want to be a father to you.'

'Who's there?' I shouted, leaping to my feet and staring around the darkened corners of the shelter. I was ready to run, when the voice came again. Clear, warm and strong, it pierced through to my heart. 'I love you and want to be a father to you. You may turn your back on me but I'll never turn my back on you. I love you.'

Stunned, I sank down again. I realised that this was no person hiding in the shelter. I wouldn't have heard them anyway, not with my deafness and the storm. This was God. I'd been running from him, shouting that I wanted nothing more to do with him, yet he was here with me in the shelter, saying he loved me and would never turn his back on me. How could that be?

I leaned back, overcome with exhaustion. I was still crying but now it felt more like grief than uncontrollable rage. God spoke again in my heart. The first time it had seemed almost physically audible, but now I became aware of little whispers passing through my mind. I could have dismissed them as imagination except that my thoughts were too incoherent in that moment to be able to express anything, least of all whispers of loving understanding.

'I want to be a father to you. You haven't yet come to me as a child comes to her father. Child, I'm not looking for your Christian duty, I'm looking for you. I don't want you to pray because that's what Christians do, I want you to pray because that's our language of love and sharing together. I want to hear what brings you joy. I want to share your tears when you are sad. I want to affirm you, to guide you, to comfort and lift you up in my love. Don't hold yourself at a distance and do the Christian things. Rather, come to me in simple trust as a little child will come to her daddy. You are that child to me and I will never leave you or forsake you.'

As these words drifted across my heart I became full of peace; it was as if all the turmoil was draining away. I was so tired yet knew that something fundamental had happened. God my Father was there with me and that was all that mattered. The thought came to me that before returning to college I should go to a couple from the church I'd just started attending. I'd visited them once and knew they lived in an area called the Meriden Estate, but had no idea of their address or how to get there. But deep inside I felt God saying that John and Amanda would help me. I said to him, 'Lord, if you really are my Father, then please help me to get there, for I am lost.'

I'd run about fifteen miles without taking any note of where I was going and by now it was gone 10 p.m. I suddenly realised how very vulnerable I was to be out alone late in the evening in such a distressed state. 'Please protect me, Father,' I prayed, and then started walking. About twenty minutes later I saw lights shining behind me and realised a bus was coming. It was virtually upon me and I was nowhere near a bus stop, so I was shocked when it stopped next to me. I glanced up at its destination and to my surprise the Meriden Estate was listed.

'Thank you for stopping for me,' I said to the driver as I climbed on. 'Single to the Meriden Estate, please.'

'That's 82p,' the driver said as he handed me the ticket.

Even in my dazed state, I knew that this was an extremely unlikely price for the distance, how could it possibly be that cheap? I wasn't sure I would have enough money as I'd only taken my small-change purse. So I was stunned when I discovered I had exactly 82p. I paid the driver and sat down.

I was shaking with tiredness and as I can never see my surroundings in the dark, I had no idea where I was or where to get off. After about fifty minutes I roused myself, suddenly alert.

'Where *is* the Meriden Estate, have I missed it?' I shouted to the driver.

'No, dear, it's the next stop,' was his reply.

Amazed again, I stepped off the bus. The rain had stopped but the roads were wet and I was standing on the edge of a big T-junction with traffic roaring in all directions, their lights dazzling. I felt disorientated and had no idea where to go. 'Lord, you got me here, please help me find their house,' I prayed silently, then started walking. With some difficulty I negotiated the busy crossing and then continued down the road that faced me. This was much quieter and, although it looked vaguely familiar, I still couldn't place it and of course didn't know the name of their road or their house number. I carried on walking in a kind of dream. By now it was heading towards midnight and all I could think of was finding somewhere safe. Everything around me was just a blur. How could I ever find their house when I had no idea what I was even looking for? Suddenly something made me pause and look harder and I felt a prompting inside me to go up to the nearest front door and ring the bell. I was scared. 'The homeowners will be so angry,' I thought. A light went on just as I was about to run. The door opened and there stood John before me. He looked astonished but held the door wide and I practically fell in. He called upstairs and then took me into the lounge, put the fire on, took my coat and wrapped a blanket round me. He disappeared into the kitchen and came back with a steaming cup of tea. He asked no questions other than to check I was unhurt.

Moments later Amanda came, her eyes sleepy, her smile so warm. She hugged me tight then showed me a nightie and dressing gown. She took me by the hand and led me upstairs. She'd made a bed for me, taking her son into their room. Lovingly she helped me out of my wet clothes and into the nightie. It was so comforting. She pulled back the duvet and there was a hot-water bottle warming the sheets. Still with no request for explanations, she helped me in, drew the duvet around me, rested her hand on my head and prayed the Father would hold me in his peace, and then quietly left the room. Amazingly, I fell asleep almost immediately.

God wants relationship above everything else

Of course this was only the beginning, not the end, of my healing journey. But it was an absolutely vital milestone along the path. It was from this moment that I began to understand the purpose of being a Christian, that above all else God wanted a real Father/daughter relationship with me. I'd already fallen into the trap of living a kind of 'to-do' list of how to be a successful Christian. I needed to pray, to read my Bible, to have fellowship with other Christians, to go to church, to serve the Lord in some way . . . already I'd been subconsciously thinking that if I managed to do all these things then I could give myself a pat on the back and think I was OK, that I'd earned my kudos and God would approve of me. But while all these things are important, even vital in order for us to grow, they can never be enough on their own; just as it can never be enough to enter into marriage solely on the basis of some kind of rule book of what constitutes a good marriage. Nothing can equal time getting to know one another, seeing what moves them or makes them afraid; being drawn to them physically, inspired by them mentally and upheld by them emotionally.

All these things we take for granted in our everyday relationships, so how can we imagine that just doing external things is enough for us as Christians? Surely, as all good things come from God, then the ability we have to truly connect with one another can only come from him? If we feel empathy with someone we meet, then who put that gift of empathy within us? When we love, fear or deeply admire someone, those are powerful emotions. The Bible says we are made in God's image (Gen. 1:27), so it follows that being able to feel things powerfully is part of that gift. So it is vital we realise that God desires a deep attachment to us, the joy of bonding and sharing together.

Through what happened that night I began to understand that God loves the whole of me, not just the 'religious' bits. He wanted me to be real with him in my prayers. He wanted to draw me in to the secrets of his heart and enable me to be privy to his purposes. The miraculous way he provided for me to get back safely, even ensuring I had enough money for the fare, were examples of his great love and care. The way that John and Amanda welcomed me that night was an example of those cords of human kindness that we were thinking about earlier. God uses his people to give us love with skin on. Sometimes a hurting child just needs Mummy or Daddy to give them a hug. That was what my lovely Father was giving me that night through John and Amanda.

Pause and reflect

- Think of any times when you've experienced God's love and care through human kindness. What was going on in your life, and how did the person reach out to you?
- How did that make you feel?
- Spend some time thanking him for showing you his loving kindness through that person. Thank him that he always cares for you and is ready to act on your behalf.

His Spirit-kiss divine

I love this version of the Song of Solomon 1:1–4 from *The Passion Translation*:

Let him smother me with kisses – his Spirit-kiss divine. So kind are your caresses, I drink them in like the sweetest wine! Your presence releases a fragrance so pleasing – over and over poured out. For your lovely name is 'Flowing Oil.' No wonder the brides-to-be adore you. Draw me into your heart. We will run away together into the king's cloud-filled chamber.

Dr Brian Simmons prayed that God's passionate love could be communicated afresh, and that is certainly happening in this passage. He has managed to combine the original poems and declarations of love between King Solomon and his beloved and the prophetic glimpses they reveal of God's heart for us in an amazing way.

'Let him smother me with kisses – his Spirit-kiss divine', cries the beloved to her lover, the king. She is not content with just a peck on the cheek like we give one another in a semblance of love. She is crying out for a real love encounter. She wants to be held by her lover and feel his kisses. She wants to be embraced and for them to be part of each other. It is one of the most expressive yet pure songs of intimate love ever penned and has the power to stir our hearts and make us long to experience love as she did. It can also make us feel uncomfortable, as it can seem irreverent to have such strong expressions of physical desire in the Bible, even more so when we realise this is also God's heart for us. But we are crazy if we divorce God from the reality of human and physical love. After all, if God hated sexual love he need never have created us with that means of experiencing deep emotion. It is the devil and our fallen nature that have made it a means of abusing or controlling others. Sex has overtaken God as the idol that everyone supposedly needs, and is satisfied by, and this breaks God's heart.

But although many Christians believe that any talk of physical love is carnal and should be avoided, the Bible itself shows that God is both Father and Lover who expresses his love with passionate longing. In chapter 1 we looked at how the father of the returning son uninhibitedly threw his arms around him, kissed him and gave him shoes, clothes and a ring . . . These would hardly be the actions of a God who hates all physical expression of love. Jesus wanted his listeners to have a true understanding which is as vital for us today as it was for them.

So how can we experience it?

Returning to the opening words from Song of Solomon 1, the beloved describes the king's kisses as kind caresses that she loves to drink in. If we apply that to God, it speaks of his desire to caress our hearts with his kindness. Not just little acts of kindness that we remember one minute and forget the next, but a kindness that thrills our hearts, inspires our minds and fills us with wonder and joy. She talks about drinking it in as if it is the sweetest wine. She is intoxicated by it and her experience makes her thirsty for more. The difficulty for us is that she has literally been with her lover and kissed him and now longs for his kisses again. But how can we truly engage with God like this when we cannot see or physically feel his touch?

The beloved's further words give us a clue:

> Your presence releases a fragrance so pleasing – over and over poured out. For your lovely name is 'Flowing Oil' (1:3).

So his constant presence with us is what enables us to experience his love. She describes it as a fragrance being poured out continuously. We cannot see his presence but it is as real, in fact even more real, than the very air we breathe which is also something we cannot see.

In John 20:27 onwards Jesus brings alive this paradox between our desire to have concrete evidence before we believe, and the truth that there is a depth of joy and blessing beyond any other when we simply believe and trust:

> Then he said to Thomas . . . 'Reach out your hand and put it into my side. Stop doubting and believe.'

> Thomas said to him, 'My Lord and my God!' (vv. 27,28 NIV).

> Jesus said to him, Because you have seen Me, Thomas, do you now believe (trust, have faith)? Blessed and happy and to be envied are those who have never seen Me and yet have believed and adhered to and trusted and relied on Me (v.29 AMPC).

Thomas was experiencing unbelief because he had not seen the physical evidence of Jesus' resurrection. So Jesus came to him and answered his heart cry for tangible evidence. Even though Jesus did not want Thomas's faith to depend on visible things, he still answered Thomas's prayer. But when Thomas joyfully responded, Jesus said, 'Blessed and happy and to be envied are those who have never seen Me and yet have believed'. Jesus was teaching Thomas that true experience comes from God, not from the things we see. When we believe God's character and his Word, a door opens for us to step into the realm of happiness and blessing that is real and lasting. It is so real that Jesus said we will be envied because of it! What an amazing promise.

Meeting with the Father

Some years ago we started running an alternative worship time at our conferences which we called 'Meeting with the Father'. We place various simple items around the room, including a table with cups and saucers representing his friendship; a bowl of water for cleansing and healing; beautiful blue and green cloths covered in sparkling stones representing the river of life; a ring representing us being his bride; a duvet representing the comfort and compassion he surrounds us with; and various lovely pictures and figures. All simple objects that we invite people to look at, touch and wrap themselves in, opening themselves up to hear God's voice of love. Apart from some readings, there is no talking, and Marilyn quietly plays the piano in the background.

One day, Joan, who had so far been very uncommunicative, decided to attend this session. Guests freely come and go so I don't take particular note of anyone's actions. As the session proceeded there was a tangible sense of the presence of God. Several of the guests were smiling, some were gently weeping, others just worshipping. I started quietly to put things away and found myself standing by the armchair which I'd draped with the duvet representing God's comfort.

Someone was still sitting there and I was about to move away, when to my astonishment Joan jumped up and with a broad smile, grabbed my hands and launched into excited speech:

'I can feel his love. Oh, I'm so warm inside. He's been smiling at me! I just want to laugh and sing. He loves me, I can feel it.'

This dear lady was overwhelmed that she had experienced God's love in such an amazing way. She had prayed in desperation before coming to the conference, 'God, please help me to feel your love.' She'd come faithfully to the meetings, joined in the worship and listened to the teaching but nothing was connecting. Then she came to this session and decided to sit in the chair with the symbolic duvet around her. She only meant to be there a couple of minutes, but realised that she was beginning to feel warm, a warmth coming from inside her heart. 'Is this you, Lord?' she asked, astonished, and suddenly saw the face of Jesus smiling at her. She had never experienced a vision before, only knowing the facts of the gospel. Now she melted inside as her pain dissolved. Experiencing the Father's love that afternoon set free her true identity. She had hardly been able to speak, so deep was her emotional pain, but now she was so excited that from then on she told everyone: 'I can feel his love, I'm all warm inside. I know what it means to love others now too.'

The Father's desire to bless us

Joan's story brings alive that the Father loves to bless us. He hears our heart's cry and our prayers and longings matter to him. As some lines in one of Marilyn's songs express:

He knows our sorrows; He holds them in His heart.
He cares, he feels, he carries every part.
He can touch our memories and heal our hurts deep inside,
Give us the strength and help we need to start again.
And all that we have been through,

He'll turn and use it for our good,
So our hearts are filled with more of his compassion.

Marilyn Baker

God wants us to know his love and be free to love him with the whole of our beings, not just in a cold, logical, dutiful way. The paradox is that just as you cannot physically see love (you may see the expression of it or hear it in people's words, but the love itself is an emotion and a choice, both of which are invisible), in the same way, you cannot see God physically, but Jesus said the most wonderful blessing comes to those who will believe even without seeing. What Joan experienced was the reality of that blessing from the Father. She cried out to him to help her know what love is, and he came and gave her joy from the inside out. As Jesus promised in John 16:23,24:

> Very truly I tell you, my Father will give you whatever you ask in my name. Until now you have not asked for anything in my name. Ask and you will receive, and your joy will be complete.

 Pause and reflect

Think about these stories of Thomas and Joan, together with this Bible verse from John.

- What does it show you about God's character that despite the smallness of their faith, God heard and answered both their prayers?
- Being honest with yourself, are you able to trust in God's love and promises even though you can't see him or an immediate change in the situation you are praying for?
- If the answer is yes, spend some time thanking the Lord that he is with you and helping you to grow in your faith.

- If the answer is 'not really', thank the Lord that he *does* love you and is working on your behalf. Ask him as 'the pioneer and perfecter of faith' (Heb. 12:2) to help you to grow and become more secure in his love for you.
- If Joan's story of experiencing God's love has resonated with you, spend time talking with your Father and ask him to help you experience what it means to be loved by him.

3

Struggling with the Concept?

Surely God is good? Surely God is love? Surely God is all-powerful? But why then do bad things happen? Why is this beautiful world tearing itself apart? And why do I feel the pain I do?

The middle-aged lady sank wearily onto the seat and sat gazing at her hands.

'Would you like to share?' I asked her gently.

She shook her head slightly but didn't look up.

'God loves you so much,' I said.

'God loves me?' she retorted, looking at me at last. 'Then why don't I ever see any sign of it? He may love others but he doesn't love me!'

This lady, who came to us for prayer at the end of a concert, was typical of many who believe in God but don't think he loves them because they haven't experienced it emotionally. The love of God seems just a nice concept which may be true for others but not for them. They feel too unworthy or have been so hurt they cannot imagine being loved.

How can God's love break through such barriers?

The power of old negative experiences

When I had my very first conversation about Christianity, after trying to take my life in the lake, Ruth told me: 'God loves you as a father.'

I longed for love and it was out of my desperate belief that I would never experience it, that I had wanted to die. So when she said that God loved me unconditionally, I was stunned. But her words that 'God loves you as a father' initially had the opposite effect. My dad died when I was 7 and although he'd been a good dad, I had no memories of him playing with me or anything in particular. I could remember him doing things with my sister but not with me. I could remember when he was ill, lying on the bed in our lounge, weak and in pain and those memories made me feel sad, so there must have been some attachment between us, but I had few father/daughter memories to make me smile as I looked back. I may just have been too young, but the fact that I do remember him being with my sister discounts that theory in my mind.

What I do know is that I had a gulf inside me that I didn't know how to fill. Then with my stepfather's arrival came everything that was belittling and crushing. The effect was to leave me with a solid, painful wall inside my heart, and although I could identify my longing to be loved, I could not accept it being connected to fatherhood.

The enemy robs us

For me, and in the lives of countless others, painful childhood experiences are used by the enemy to rob us of a heart understanding of God's Father love. These are real wounds causing real barriers, but God can transform those hurts and will do so as we work in partnership with him. Our own sinfulness and blindness to the truth also create barriers to us experiencing his love. You can see Jesus' longing to free those who were trapped in a negative or sinful lifestyle or even in destructive self-righteousness, like the older brother in the prodigal son story. Jesus compassionately responded to people's despair in such a way that his critics could not help but see God's love in action. He wanted their hearts to be cracked open and changed but they would not always let themselves respond, so their hearts remained hard. In Matthew 13:14,15 Jesus said about them, quoting from a prophecy in Isaiah:

> You will be ever hearing but never understanding; you will be ever seeing but never perceiving. For this people's heart has become

calloused; they hardly hear with their ears, and they have closed their eyes. Otherwise they might see with their eyes, hear with their ears, understand with their hearts and turn, and I would heal them.

I find this passage heart-breaking as I see its truth daily in my own life as much as I do in others. Even now my heart is so hard at times and I won't allow myself to see things differently and so receive his healing. The passage shows we are meant to live our ordinary lives with our spiritual ears and eyes open to his voice. In my everyday life I often become aware that God wants me to listen to him, but I easily ignore that inner nudging and so fail to perceive his heart for me or for someone else. Each time that happens, I make myself more blind and deaf to his love. As someone who is literally deaf and has very poor vision, I would do anything to hear properly if that were possible, and I know all sorts of things would open up to me if I could see more. I cannot change my physical problems but I can change my spiritual blindness and deafness simply by choosing to have a receptive heart to God's love.

My painful experiences may say 'there's no point in opening your heart, he'll just let you down'. That cynical lack of trust traps us into believing that he's as bad as all the hard things we've experienced. We can attribute so much authority to them that they can become like God to us, seemingly more powerful than anything else. We then in effect hide ourselves away, closing off any likelihood that God will truly love us.

But as Solomon said in Proverbs 3:5, God calls us to:

Trust in the LORD with all your heart and lean not on your own understanding.

Let's choose to trust in what God says and does, not in our past negative experiences.

Marilyn struggled for years because her dad, in his bitterness about her blindness, would repeatedly say, 'You'll just be a nuisance to people if you ask for help all the time.' That word 'nuisance' was like an arrow in Marilyn's heart and she became very nervous of asking for help. But a counsellor encouraged her to lay down that wrong view of herself. As Marilyn prayed, God showed her that far from being a nuisance, he wanted her to see herself as a blessing to others, even those she asked for help. I hadn't known about this, but afterwards was out shopping with Marilyn and popped to some other shops while Marilyn went into a frozen-food store. She felt nervous as she knew she would need to get an assistant to help her, but God spoke to her, saying, 'Remember I told you about viewing yourself as a blessing? Ask for this help with confidence that you *will* be a blessing not a nuisance to the assistant.' So Marilyn tried to be relaxed and enjoy her time. I came into the shop to meet her just as they were finishing at the checkout. The assistant was laughing and had obviously enjoyed being with Marilyn, so I, knowing nothing of what had been going on in Marilyn's heart, told her as we went out, 'I could see you were a real blessing to that assistant, you made her day and she was so happy to help you!' Marilyn was amazed and realised how much the Lord wanted her to take that truth to heart.

 Pause and reflect

- Are there any times when you know you have resisted listening to God or opening up to his love? Why do you think that was?
- Spend a few minutes saying sorry to him, and ask him to help you be open to receive all he wants to give you.
- Thinking of Marilyn's story, ask the Holy Spirit if there are any negatives you've believed about yourself as a result of others' words or actions.
- Ask him to set you free from their power and to show you his truth instead. Ask him to help you apply it in your life, like Marilyn thinking of herself as a blessing to that shop assistant, not a nuisance.

We may feel that it is impossible to know God when we are wounded, but God has made our hearts, that is, our innermost beings, with the capacity to know him, to hear his voice and experience his love. Our hurts, sins and wrong beliefs may stunt that capacity but can never annihilate it. In the same way, we can stunt our ability to make wise decisions if we always rely on stronger people to decide for us. But as soon as we start to think for ourselves, our brains will start to roll into gear. So God wants to encourage us that we can experience his love. We may not know how to do it, but the ability to connect with him is what he has created us for.

The Spirit of adoption

As well as giving us an inner capacity to experience him, God has also given us the amazing gift of his own Spirit who has the mission to make known within us that we are God's adopted children. Listen to what Paul teaches us in Romans 8:14,15:

> For those who are led by the Spirit of God are the children of God. The Spirit you received does not make you slaves, so that you live in fear again; rather, the Spirit you received brought about your adoption to sonship. And by him we cry, '*Abba*, Father.'

In his book, *My Father's Tears: The Cross and the Father's Love*, Dr Mark Stibbe, who was himself adopted as a baby, shares how the Holy Spirit gave him a heart revelation that God loved him as a son:

> In the end it was an encounter with the Holy Spirit that took this picture of God as Father from my head to my heart. Through the Spirit of adoption, my heart was inflamed with a stunning and entirely new revelation: *Thanks to what Jesus has done at Calvary, we can come to see that God is the Father who has adopted us as his royal sons and daughters, and with Spirit-ignited hearts we can know him relationally and speak to him personally.*[1]

Mark teaches: 'On five occasions the apostle Paul had used the word *huiothesia*, literally "the placing of a son", translated in most versions as "adoption". Further research uncovered that Paul had been using a picture from the Roman world. He was a Roman citizen so Roman adoptions were familiar to him.'

In effect, through this picture of Roman adoptive customs, Paul was teaching us that God has completely removed us from the enslaving control of all that has gone before and placed us in his royal family and lineage. We have literally been made royal sons and daughters. In doing so he has also totally cancelled every debt and removed it from us forever.

 Pause and reflect

- What does it mean to you that God has adopted you to be his royal son or daughter?
- Think of something that is precious to you, like your spouse or child, your home, a pet, a family heirloom . . .
- What emotions are you aware of as you think of this precious thing?
- Try to imagine now what emotions fill God's heart as he thinks of you, his beloved adopted child.
- Write in your journal all that comes to mind and spend time thanking him for his love in choosing you.

The true Father

When I was a child and life was becoming very difficult, I went through a phase of hoping desperately that I'd been adopted. I fantasised that certain teachers would suddenly disclose that I was their long-lost daughter. I even searched my mum's desk trying to find 'proof' of my adoption, but all I found was my birth certificate which showed unequivocally that I was indeed my parents' natural daughter. It was crazy because you only had to see my mum and me together to know we were related. I also knew that my mum really did love me and was doing her best, and I loved her and the rest of the family too, but a big part of me felt different and being singled out for abuse didn't help.

Because of my fraught experiences it seemed impossible to imagine how I could actually become secure in knowing God's love. Yet step by step he made himself known, touched me with his love and brought healing to my heart.

The poem I shared in the Prologue describes the hopes I'd had as a child for a loving father to nurture me into the woman I was created to be. These hopes are buried deep in our subconscious and both our parents are called to fulfil them in their own unique ways. We all have such longings, even if we never acknowledge them, but when they are dismissed, we become deeply wounded. In the poem I share how my loving heavenly Father started to transform these deep wounds of shame and rejection into love and empathy for others.

Take a few moments to re-read my Prologue poem and pray about your own buried childhood longings with your heavenly Father, who is with you right now to bring you that same joy of inner transformation.

A healing picture

As I am writing this chapter, I sense the Father's deep compassion for someone. You feel as if you are buried in a concrete tomb. You have been robbed of love for so long that you can no longer feel anything. It's as if that very concrete has become who you are. You have no hope in God being able to help you. I saw him reaching out to you and tearing the slabs of concrete away. He becomes bruised and cut but he doesn't give up because his love for you consumes him. He is weeping over all the pain you have experienced and as his tears hit the concrete they melt it, each tear creating a furrow. All the furrows join together and the power of the concrete is weakened until it all breaks apart. You are lying in the broken shards still not believing you are free, but he embraces you and there is nothing to stop him lifting you out, and you see his eyes are full of joy as he frees you from that tomb forever.

◤ Pause and reflect

- Spend time reflecting on this prophetic picture.
- Are you aware of areas in your own life that have turned your longings and hopes into concrete?

- Know that your heavenly Father is showing you this because he loves you and understands your pain but longs to release you from its hold over your life. Thank him for the truth it depicts of his power to free you, and ask him to fulfil it in your life.
- Thank him that he has created you to know and experience his love and that you trust him to fulfil your love longings.
- If you become aware of memories that are too painful to deal with alone, don't be afraid to seek help. Both prayer ministry and Christian counselling are invaluable in aiding us to step through our traumas into wholeness.

Being real but allowing God to change us

In the following verses from Psalm 73 it is clear that the psalmist, Asaph, is experiencing similar issues. He starts by declaring confidently: 'Surely God is good to Israel, to those who are pure in heart', but then continues; 'But as for me, my feet had almost slipped; I had nearly lost my foothold. For I envied the arrogant when I saw the prosperity of the wicked' (vv. 1–3).

Like many of us, Asaph desperately wants to believe that God is good, but feels overwhelmed by the struggles godly people experience. He is looking with human understanding at the lives of those around him. They don't have faith and even publicly mock God, yet they don't appear to have any problems. They even carry out acts of violence without any backlash; in fact, they seem to gain in popularity. How can this be? Asaph sees the difference between these people who are seemingly immune to God's judgement, and others who are trying to live godly lives yet suffer constant pain, which mocks the concept of a loving God. Asaph describes it graphically as a struggle he is personally experiencing:

> Surely in vain I have kept my heart pure and have washed my hands in innocence. All day long I have been afflicted, and every morning brings new punishments (vv. 13,14).

Like us, Asaph refrains from sharing his doubts with other believers as he does not want to pull them down with his own disillusionment. But in trying to bury his feelings, his confusion becomes even stronger:

> When my heart was grieved and my spirit embittered . . . it troubled me deeply . . . I was senseless and ignorant; I was a brute beast before you (vv. 21,16,22).

I find this psalm a great comfort, as it expresses the eternal mystery we all struggle with. We know that God is good; he is a loving Father; he can heal and in him is all power to do amazing works. We know that Jesus' death and resurrection comprise a total work of salvation, forgiveness, eternal life and adoption into his family for all who believe. We know that he promises to give us joy beyond anything else. We know all this, but it seems so hard to equate those truths meaningfully with the chaotic way we experience life sometimes and the mystery of why terrible things can happen. If God's love and promises are real, why is life so hard?

But God *is* the answer

No Christian cliché will provide anything near to a satisfactory answer but nevertheless God really *is* the answer. Not religion and trusting in doctrines but God himself and the door he has opened for us to be in relationship with him. In this same psalm, Asaph shows us the key:

> When I tried to understand all this, it troubled me deeply till I entered the sanctuary of God; then I understood their final destiny (vv. 16,17).

By 'entered the sanctuary of God', Asaph wasn't talking about going into a church, which would be simplistic to an extreme. He was referring to the secret place where he and God could communicate together as friends; finding God in the sanctuary of his own heart and hearing him speak words of revelation and understanding.

Such words would transform his attitude and enable him to trust God from the depth of his being, no longer just mental assent but heart experience.

> Yet I am always with you; you hold me by my right hand. You guide me with your counsel, and afterwards you will take me into glory. Whom have I in heaven but you? And earth has nothing I desire besides you. My flesh and my heart may fail, but God is the strength of my heart and my portion for ever (vv. 23–26).

Asaph moves from confusion and hopelessness to something completely different. He has heard God speaking, not just superficial clichés like we sometimes come out with, but words that have imparted a fundamental joy and security. Worries about his physical struggles are melting away as he says, 'My flesh and my heart may fail, but God is the strength of my heart and my portion for ever.' His new God-given understanding is empowering him to see from a different perspective.

Any of us who experience physical struggles will know you can't just ignore them. I am very fortunate that apart from on brief occasions, I very rarely experience physical pain, but I know those who do and see how all-consuming that pain is. In a similar way my deafness is hard to ignore as are any mobility or visual problems that others contend with.

Asaph began the psalm caught up in struggles which humanly he couldn't extricate himself from, but by the end has entered a new dimension of joy, peace and worship instead of despair. To me, the phrase which sums up this transition is: 'You guide me with your counsel'. We often think of God's counsel in relation to decisions we need to make. But while he does have a plan for us, he is far more interested in our hearts and his ultimate plan is that we become more and more like Jesus. God loves to give us counsel that will bring the revelation of his Father love from our heads into our hearts, and to show us areas in our inner lives that need his transforming touch.

A personal illustration

Recently I had a dream, which isn't a very usual way for me to hear the Lord. The dream wasn't of anything exotic, in fact it was a very mundane event, but it left me with a deep sense of melancholy. I was visiting someone I know well and yet the house seemed totally different. I felt lost and displaced. I was wandering round the rooms with no clear sense of why I was there or of being connected to anyone. I went into one room and there were dirty cups and plates lying around so I decided to wash up as it would give me a role. However, when I turned away momentarily, I found on turning back that a young man was now washing up. He didn't speak to me and I felt invisible, so I went into another room and found a big group of people rehearsing a dance. I felt sad because I lead dance workshops and would have liked to have joined in. But again, I felt totally invisible. No one was unkind and nothing was horrid about the dream, but when I woke up, the prevailing feeling was of loss. I had no idea why I'd dreamt like this, but as I had, unusually for me, remembered it, I decided to ask the Lord what it meant. I thought maybe he wanted me to intercede for someone who was feeling lonely, but it was these thoughts that came to my heart: 'The dream arose out of your inner sense of being and what you feed it with. You allow yourself to believe that you are not really wanted and that it doesn't matter if you are present or not. You have caused yourself, therefore, to be not present to a great many people and things that I have brought into your life to give you joy. You are living in a way that I have not intended for I made you to live in fullness of life and joy. You need to come out of your self-imposed prison and start to live life with me.'

I was quite shocked by this revelation. I am certainly not miserable all the time and I really do know that I am loved both by God and by the people around me. However, as I reflected I realised that there is an inner part of me that does feel very alone and often quite superfluous, as if I am there but not there. My deafness doesn't help as it inevitably puts me on the fringe of what's happening. But this feeling goes much deeper than being deaf and is probably more to do with my early rejections and the way I had come to believe so many negative things about myself. God has healed so much over the years, but he alone can truly see what is going on at the deepest levels of our hearts. So he came to me in this dream which stirred up my buried emotions and then gave me his counsel so I could know what the dream was telling me and what he wanted me to do to step into deeper wholeness. Like Asaph, I now feel full of joy that the Lord has spoken to me in this way and given me the key for heart healing.

The key

God sees every detail of our lives and knows how we need our inner attitudes transforming. The key is to enter 'his sanctuary' like Asaph did. Often on waking, I just rush into getting ready for the day, but if I had done that I would have forgotten that dream very quickly. Even when we have a regular quiet time, we can tackle it with the attitude that we need to read a certain amount of the Bible and pray. We may pray quite beautifully for others but not make any space for him to touch our own hearts. He is our Father, whose desire is always to have real communication with us in the midst of our everyday lives. Listen afresh to these very familiar but heart-searching words from Revelation 3:20:

> Here I am! I stand at the door and knock. If anyone hears my voice and opens the door, I will come in and eat with that person, and they with me.

He daily knocks on the door of our hearts, wanting us to welcome him to be with us in the midst of everything. He wants to relax with us and draw us into the kind of intimacy that a mealtime with a friend depicts. He doesn't force this desire upon us, as true love never forces; instead, he knocks. This is why we are called to live in partnership with him, making choices to believe in his love and expecting him to speak and 'guide us with his counsel.'

✦ Pause and reflect

- Read through Psalm 73 and ask the Lord to show you any conscious or subconscious areas of your life where you find it hard to believe that he is truly good.
- Ask him 'to guide you with his counsel' for any new understanding he wants you to grow in.
- Thank him for any insights and ask him to plant them like seeds in your heart. Thinking of how God used my dreams to show me my inner need, ask him to remind you of any way he has spoken similarly to you. Were you aware of it at the time? What has been the fruit? (If you don't know, ask him to tell you, you may be amazed at what comes to mind!)
- Spend some time worshipping him.

He draws you with his love

> The Lord appeared from of old to me [Israel], saying, Yes, I have loved you with an everlasting love; therefore with loving-kindness have I drawn you and continued My faithfulness to you (Jer. 31:3 AMPC).

I love this word 'drawn'. It is an old-fashioned word implying, amongst other things, the use of a steady force to bring something close. God is telling us that the steady force of his everlasting love constantly draws us to himself. It's as if we are a treasure that fills his mind and heart. But what does this mean in real terms? Have you ever been drawn towards someone? Everything they say or even just their sheer presence heightens your awareness of them. There may be a crowd in the room but you are only aware of the one person. If they move, your gaze is drawn to their whereabouts like a pin is drawn to a magnet. There may be twenty people between you and them, but when you catch each other's eye, happiness fills your hearts.

So, the word 'drawn' signifies God's emotional longing for us and our equally emotional response, that we will recognise that this is something that we deeply desire for ourselves.

One of the factors he uses to draw us in this way is what the Bible describes as 'loving-kindness'. Kindness is something tangible that we all experience. Do you ever stop to think when someone shows you kindness, that it is God working through that person to draw you to himself? The depressed lady I described at the start of this chapter couldn't believe God loved her, as she felt she'd never experienced it. Maybe she was expecting that love experience to be like a kind of 'out of body' religious ecstasy. This is what so many of us believe, myself included at times. But God knows us. When you know someone you know the things that make them tick, the things that warm or thrill them or that turn them cold. The most mundane or even difficult instances in your life may be things that behind the scenes he has been using to draw you to himself. Let me share a personal example . . .

Hats and cream cakes

When I first went to college and was living in lodgings with Helen, I couldn't understand why anyone would believe in a God who seemed totally cut off from the realities of everyday life. Realising that Helen had been brought up in the church I dismissed her faith as a crutch. But a couple of weeks after starting college, Helen invited me to go to church with her and surprisingly I agreed. Her church required women to wear hats. I found this highly embarrassing, and of course I had no understanding of church doctrine and how that can vary be-tween denominations, or even within them. So I didn't understand the need for a hat, nor did I understand any of the service. I remember the sermon and the prayers both taking a long time. I got through them by trying to count the marks on the walls and seeing how many marks each prayer or the sermon took. Helen was mortified when I told her as she'd been praying for God to touch me, but to me it was all a slightly hilarious waste of time. But after the service we went to tea with an older couple who had a cosy lounge, soft armchairs and who made us a lovely tea complete with home-made cream cakes. I loved that part of the exercise and, amazingly, the following week, when Helen had gone home for the weekend, I decided to go to the church on my own. I even searched Helen's drawers for her hat and then got the bus into town and set off in the direction I thought we'd walked the week before. But it's a large town and my sense of direction is nil. I couldn't find the church and, after spending an hour getting funny looks when I asked for directions, I realised I wasn't going to make it and certainly wouldn't be getting my cream tea again. I went back home and re-placed Helen's hat, which by now was rather battered as I'd squashed it into my bag.

For a long time after that I dismissed my surprising search for the church as greed, in wanting another free cream tea. This was what I told Helen, but what I hadn't realised was that it was Father God's love that was drawing me there. He was behind my being chosen to live out in lodgings with a Christian student. He was behind her asking me to go to church and the old couple inviting us for tea. He knew the lack of safety I'd experienced and that the tea and atmosphere of love in their home would tap into something deep within me. At the time I thought my decision to return was just me being greedy, but he knew me and was using this 'pull' of the cream tea to lead me to the Father's heart.

God has always wanted you to be his own

Think of these words from Ephesians 1:3–5:

> Everything heaven contains has already been lavished upon us as a love gift from our wonderful heavenly Father, the Father of our Lord Jesus Christ – all because he sees us wrapped into Christ . . . And he chose us to be his very own, joining us to himself even before he laid the foundation of the universe! . . . For it was always his plan to adopt us as his delightful children' (précis of TPT).

'He chose us to be his very own, joining us to himself even before he laid the foundation of the universe!' It is because of verses like these that I can write such statements as: he was behind my being invited to tea with that old couple.

This passage in Ephesians gives us a glimpse of God's amazing love for us. He who is complete in himself wants us to belong to him. He wanted our love and relationship from the beginning. So much so that he set plans in motion for his Son to save us even before any history had taken place. Only God the Father can fill the void in each of our hearts.

 Pause and reflect

- Spend a few moments looking back over your life, especially to that period when you responded to God's love for you, either for the first time or in a deepening understanding of what you had grown up believing.
- Can you remember any choices you made which at the time seemed unlikely or surprising?
- Can you remember any encounters with Christians which had an impact on you?
- Can you remember any feeling of longing or a pull to experience something? You may not have known what it was, but can you remember it being there?
- What was the determining factor that led you to respond to God?
- Thank him for all he did to draw you into relationship with himself.

4

Laying the Foundations

By the grace God has given me, I laid a foundation as a wise builder . . . But each one should build with care. . . . If anyone builds on this foundation using gold, silver, costly stones, wood, hay or straw, their work will be shown for what it is.

1 Cor. 3:10–13

What are your foundations like?

Sometimes I enjoy watching TV shows about families trying to build the house of their dreams or redesign their present homes. Programmes such as Channel 4's *Grand Designs* show complex structures being built from scratch, conforming to a picture that the owner carries in his head. Not being practical myself, I get hooked at the apparent ease with which walls go up, complex electrics are installed and everything completed within a few hours. I always find it inspiring that something beautiful can emerge out of such chaos.

A vital thing seems to be getting the foundations right. Whether they are building a mansion or a cottage, the foundations need to be deep enough to support it against all the destructive forces of time and weather. In a documentary, many families were left in dangerously unstable homes with sham foundations that had nowhere near the required depth. The families were devastated with many left in debt because of cowboy builders.

I sensed God speaking to me about how such building or restoring of houses is a picture of his work in our lives. He delights in bringing his perfect plans to birth and lovingly working on every unfolding detail.

But he also grieves at the devastation wrought when, like those rogue builders, key people in our lives abuse their positions, resulting in shattered foundations and lives full of cracks and debris. As I reflected, the need for strong foundations became a significant spiritual key, as God showed me the importance of us building foundations of love and truth into our lives.

Listen to Jesus' parable about the wise and foolish builders in Matthew 7:24–27:

> Therefore everyone who hears these words of mine and puts them into practice is like a wise man who built his house on the rock. The rain came down, the streams rose, and the winds blew and beat against that house; yet it did not fall, because it had its foundation on the rock. But everyone who hears these words of mine and does not put them into practice is like a foolish man who built his house on sand. The rain came down, the streams rose, and the winds blew and beat against that house, and it fell with a great crash.

We are all buildings in progress and the Designer has an awe-inspiring plan, but the key for that to happen is that our foundations are built on the rock of his Word. In order for his Word to really bear fruit we need to read it, hear it, trust in it and put it into practice. If we don't, and if we persist in allowing our experiences or the vacillating opinions of society to become the foundations of what we believe, the effect will be the equivalent of our house being built on sand. Sand represents our fears, doubts, uncertainty, indecisiveness and overdependency on the opinions of others.

What kind of words do you live by?

Do you know how much your heavenly Father respects you? Maybe your life experiences have left you with a deep lack of self-worth and you feel a failure? Or preface every conversation with words like 'I can't do that' or 'I am useless at that'? This kind of self-talk is even more destructive when you progress to saying 'I am a failure' or 'I am useless'. Such words cause the foundations of our lives to be sand rather than rock. In repeatedly speaking out or even thinking words like these, we endow them with such spiritual authority that they can literally become our identity.

A personal illustration

One of the many negative words that my stepfather constantly shouted at me was that I was lazy. I loved reading (and still do). Mum would call me for dinner and as I came downstairs, I would hear my stepfather ranting about how lazy I was, that all I did was sit with my nose in a book, that I was a useless good-for-nothing. He never seemed to understand that often I'd be reading to study for my exams, as well as for the love of books. I couldn't argue with him, he would just shout manically. Some people find that hearing themselves described negatively drives them to prove that negativity wrong; for example, becoming workaholics out of the fear of being thought lazy. For others, the words create hopelessness because in being spoken so often they become your identity, and you start to act in a way that fulfils them. I am not lazy, but sometimes the hopelessness of not being able to fight back in my childhood still seeps into everything. I may think, 'the garden needs weeding', but a languor will come over me with the certainty that even if I try, I will do it wrong. Then I'll feel too afraid to try and, in the end, will do nothing and later get upset with myself for being lazy. I am living out of the wrong foundations.

 Pause and reflect

Take a moment and reflect on this extract from one of Marilyn's songs, 'Think About These Things'. The lyrics urge us to consciously feed on all that is good and lovely, praiseworthy and beautiful, for these are the things that will release us into freedom. Out of what we feed ourselves with, whether good or bad, there will be foundations built, habits formed and a destiny created. So what will we choose to feed on?

Whatever is good; whatever is lovely, think about these things . . .
The things you feed your mind upon, will shape all you say and do.
If you say and do things often enough, they form habits that are part of you.
And habits formed whether good or bad,
Shape your character, who you will be,
And from your character springs a lifestyle, and then a destiny,
Yes everything you're choosing will pull you down or make you strong.
Because you're made in God's image, made for eternity.
So don't make less of yourself, don't just throw it away . . .

Marilyn Baker

Extract taken from the song 'Think About These Things' by Marilyn Baker (Authentic).
Copyright © 2004, CN Productions.*

Our choices of what we think about ourselves, what we dwell upon and what we say are all so important, and our ability to build the right foundations in our lives depend on them. There is a very thought-provoking verse in Proverbs 18:21:

Death and life are in the power of the tongue, and they who indulge in it shall eat the fruit of it [for death or life] (AMPC).

Our thoughts and words make a difference. If we have had negatives spoken over us and then constantly think about those words and speak them out in our conversations, then part of us will die: our self-esteem, our adventurousness, our boldness in prayer, our ability to love, our joy and wonder. But if we choose to focus upon God's love and speak out his truths about us, his life will penetrate to our very depths and transform us.

A healing dialogue

The following is a poem I wrote when I was praying one day while in a garden. For some reason all the lovely colours of the foliage created a deep sense of melancholy. I found myself talking to God about my feelings and writing his answers down. Afterwards I was amazed how poetic it was, but also at its depth of truth. Read it slowly and reflect on the answers Father God gave me. They may speak to you too.

Creator Without Apology

Lord I feel such a sense of apology;
I see the glory of the autumn leaves
Revealing the gold of your glory.
I see the beauty of the plants,
And feel the joy of your creation.
That you put the stamp of who you are,
On every living thing, without apology.
An extravagance of colour, texture and smell.
Each tiny leaf or bud itself, gladly, without apology.
But then I sensed you say to me:
'In as far as these things reflect my beauty,
They are nothing compared to you.'
And I recoiled, for how could that be?
'It's my greatest longing to reflect your glory,
Yet I cannot seem to think of me without apology.
Deep down I feel like a jumble of things thrown together
Rather haphazardly.
A kind of mistake, neither this nor that, an embarrassment,
Has become my identity.'
You say, 'Could I have created my child with less passion and joy,
To be less beautiful than a flower, a bird, or a tree?
As beautiful as they are and revealing of my splendour,
They cannot talk with me.

But I made you to be part of me
And thus, to reveal my beauty.'
But the shame that runs through me like thread through a cloth,
Draws me down and away,
If I were anyone else I would accept that as true,
But not as me.
But deep in my heart I hear him call 'Tracy, Tracy.'
And his voice is full of love reaching in to me.
I long to uncurl from my foetal ball
And let him draw the shame thread from me.
And he hears my longing and speaks again
'Child, accept the gift I have made you to be.'
And this is the door that I need to go through
Into all that God has for me.
It seems heavy and impenetrable, but he has offered me the key.
I don't know how to use it, for the shame thread blinds and binds me,
And accepting myself as a gift, seems an impossibility.
'What about my deafness and lack of ability
Surely they are not gifts, they constantly rob me.'
And in my anger I echo the words I've heard
'I'm just pathetic, a useless liability.'
But his voice comes again, warm and even laughing
'Child don't let your wounds blind you to the artist
And limit the richness of my creativity.'
And I hear and am stilled and stand at that door.
And realise he is standing there with me.
And I turn and ask, as no plant can do,
'Please forgive me my blindness and for mocking your art
Please help me take and use that key.
Because I really do want to be free.'[1]

 Pause and reflect

- What was the melancholic voice in my heart trying to tell me?
- How did God answer?

- What was the key he wanted me to use?
- What is God saying to you through this?
- Are there any steps you need to take? How you think about yourself or what you say about yourself?
- Put a CD on of uplifting worship music and spend some time basking in his love for you.

The true foundation

There is a story in Matthew 3:16,17 that thrills me and unearths an empowering key for us to step into the deepest foundations of joy and inner security. It's the story of what happened to Jesus right at the beginning of his ministry. At this stage he'd never astonished people with his teaching or performed any miracles. To all intents and purposes Jesus was an ordinary man, doing an ordinary job as a carpenter and living out the extra responsibilities that came with being the eldest son. Yet the Holy Spirit came upon him when he was baptised and, before all the people, God affirmed Jesus as his beloved son.

> After his baptism, as Jesus came up out of the water, the heavens were opened and he saw the Spirit of God descending like a dove and settling on him. And a voice from heaven said, 'This is my dearly loved Son, who brings me great joy' (NLT).

Another translation says: 'This is My Son, whom I love; this is the Apple of My eye; with Him I am well pleased' (THE VOICE).

God delighted in affirming his son and wanted Jesus to know he was dearly loved. He wasn't afraid to express great pleasure in him, not because of his achievements but just because he was his son. This is a vital foundation that every person needs, and the earlier it is given to us the better. Every newborn baby needs to know that it is loved and wanted. A baby has no ability to rationalise. They experience the world through sensation, and slowly begin to develop an understanding of life as those sensations are internalised and become part of their expectations. So a baby that is smiled upon, cuddled, fed, changed, comforted, spoken to, bathed and sung over will begin to associate those pleasant sensations with the person giving them, and will slowly begin to build up the understanding that: I am loved; I am cared for; I am wanted; I am all right as I am. These become foundations that secure their heart as surely as any house's foundation secures that building. Listen to the prayer Paul prayed for the Ephesians in Ephesians 3:17–19:

> And I pray that you, *being rooted and established in love*, may have power, together with all the Lord's holy people, to grasp how wide and long and high and deep is the love of Christ, and to know this love that surpasses knowledge (emphasis mine).

Paul was praying that we would be 'rooted and established in love'. In other words, that God's love would become our heart foundation out of which would come the power to really experience it. Striving to live a perfect life won't get us there. Our responsibility is to accept God's love and seek for it to become the way we think and feel about ourselves. The following is a story of how the Lord began to minister good foundations to a friend, Fiona, through a spiritual exercise.

Fiona's story

> This started with a card from my daughter. She wrote:

> 'I feel God is saying to you: "Dear One, will you take one week and each day sit down and ask me what my three favourite things are about you and write them down. Then at the end of the week read them aloud to yourself before you go to sleep? Lots of love, Papa God."'

> This was in November 2013 and a week later I started. I asked him to show me three of his favourite things about me. He said: 'My openness of heart, my compassion, and my kindness.'

> As I wrote these down, a voice inside told me they were lies. I prayed 'Father why can't I accept what you tell me?' He said, 'It's because your

inner lens causes you to only see your flaws, but that's why I put you in Christ, remember my love is never based on your performance.'

Then I got a picture of a little girl gleefully standing in her daddy's shoes which are way too big for her. I felt that Father said the shoes represent those things that he loves about me but which I feel I'm not deserving of. He said, 'Step into my shoes because I will fill the gaps where your own feet are too small.'

Day two, and three more things came to mind: my beauty, my faithfulness, my radical desire to go all out for God. I felt the Holy Spirit was saying: 'With these true words, I'm slowly filling up another part of your Daddy's shoes, so they will fit you.'

Day three, my steadfastness, my continuing desire for the Lord, and my desire to be right. 'But Lord,' I protested, 'I find that I fail in all these things, almost at the first post.' He replied, 'You are not listening to the right voice and yes if it was left to you alone, you would never develop these qualities in your own strength. But I love you as you are, just like you love your children. You don't expect perfection, you just love them for trying. So you must accept that I love you just as you are.'

The next day our conversation continued with me saying, 'I call you Father but I don't know it in my heart. Please show me what it looks like to be a daughter who brings you joy. I repent of struggling to believe these things, but Lord, if you say it, then that settles it.'

He said, 'Today it's your creativity, your love of nature, and your love for your children and others.'

I was still struggling but he said, 'Stand still, you can't run before you can walk. This is a process and you are my precious daughter. You need nurture which I will give you. Allow yourself time for this process to happen. Allow yourself to just be in my shoes.'

So that was in 2013 and I know that I'm still working on all this. I pray that Father will bless others through this conversation and revelation. I have since had a grandchild, and one of the pictures I was sent shows him putting one of his tiny little feet into his daddy's big slipper.[2]

I love the simplicity yet real power of this exercise and am looking forward to spending time with my Father like Fiona did, asking him to tell me what his favourite things are about me. It doesn't have to be exactly three phrases, the key is that we expect to hear him and believe that he wants to plant seeds of truth in our hearts. He has given us ears to hear and tells us 'My sheep listen to my voice' (John 10:27). It doesn't matter how long you've been one of his sheep, he loves you and has given you all you need to hear him. His voice may come like the whisper of an idea in your heart; or you may suddenly think of a verse from the Bible or a line from a hymn. Maybe something beautiful or evocative in creation will draw your attention, or a conversation with thoughts 'replying' to your own prayers like Fiona experienced. Remember, God's desire is to root you in his love.

Think of this short conversation that Jesus had with Nathanael in John 1:47–49:

> When Jesus saw Nathanael approaching, he said of him, 'Here truly is an Israelite in whom there is no deceit.'
>
> 'How do you know me?' Nathanael asked.
>
> Jesus answered, 'I saw you while you were still under the fig-tree before Philip called you.'
>
> Then Nathanael declared, 'Rabbi, you are the Son of God; you are the king of Israel.'

There is more to their conversation, but the thing to notice was that as soon as he saw him, Jesus spoke a grace truth over Nathanael, describing him as a true Israelite. This astonished Nathanael, just as it often astonishes us to hear how God sees us. Then when Jesus said he had seen Nathanael under the fig tree (which must have been by revelation, not by literally bumping into him), Nathanael was catapulted into faith and changed from the inside out. This is the power of encountering God and realising how all-encompassing his love is.

Pause and reflect

- Find somewhere comfortable and have your journal, pen and Bible to hand.
- Thank the Lord that he is with you as your loving Father.
- Ask him to show you some things he loves about you. You may get a simple word or phrase drop into your mind, or an awareness of what makes you unique, or a Bible verse. The key is that his words will be life-giving. If any come that are negative or belittling, you can be sure they are from the devil, not from God.
- Thank him and ask him to plant these truths into your heart like seeds that will bear fruit.
- Pray in a similar way over the next few days.
- Start thinking of yourself in the light of what God has shown you, speaking his truths aloud over yourself.
- Ask him to help you to live out of these truths instead of the old negatives.

God wants each of us to have that same sure foundation

Returning to what we looked at earlier about Jesus' baptism and the way God affirmed him there, it's vital that we realise that God wants to affirm us in the same way. The Bible says:

> As the Father has loved me, so have I loved you. Now remain in my love (John 15:9).

> I have loved you with an everlasting love; I have drawn you with unfailing kindness (Jer. 31:3).

> . . . so that they may be brought to complete unity. Then the world will know that you sent me and have loved them even as you have loved me (John 17:23).

As hard as we may find it to accept, these and many other verses tell us that we are loved by God with the same everlasting love as Jesus.

We are brothers and sisters with Jesus. Do you believe this? Humanly I find it impossible. I mean, how can it be true? Jesus is perfect. He is literally part of the Godhead, so how can we claim that God loves us when we mess up so easily? Yet the fact remains, God loves us to the same degree as he loves Jesus. We too are his beloved children. What we must do is accept that truth. As we read in 1 John 3:1:

> See what great love the Father has lavished on us, that we should be called children of God! And that is what we are!

Lavish

This short verse is a wonderful example of a strong foundational truth for us to take hold of. Think of that word 'lavished'; it is saying that God pours his love upon you and spreads the message that you are his beloved child over every part of your life.

In our conferences I sometimes compare this word 'lavish' to the way I enjoy spreading butter on my toast. I never put just enough to cover the slice; instead I spread it on lavishly because I love the taste. Fortunately, butter is no longer considered to be a health hazard so I go for it and thoroughly enjoy it.

In the same way, John is saying that God loves us, not just in a piffling, tolerant way, but that he pours his love upon us. He cannot do enough for us. He gives it to us abundantly and extravagantly, not just forgiving one sin but every sin we may ever commit; not just providing for one need in our lives, but for *all* our needs; not just accept us because of the cross, but making us his beloved children and heirs . . .

 Pause and reflect

- What does that word 'lavish' mean to you?
- Can you see in your own habits or in those of someone close to you how you might act lavishly? For example, giving gifts to someone you love, using a certain spice in your cooking or praising someone.

- Bearing that in mind, what does it show you that God lavishes his love on *you*? What is God saying to you through this word?
- Talk to him about any insights that come, and spend time basking in his lavish love.

The greatest need in the world

We are wanted and loved. This is one of the greatest messages needed in our modern world. I'm not undermining the suffering of previous generations; the tears, silent screams and losses of each generation have been beyond terrible. But God has chosen for us to live now, and one of the hallmarks of this age is the scale of fatherlessness across the world.

In the West, a vast number of children have no concept of a loving two-parent family. For many it's the norm to live with siblings they're not related to and to have 'daddies' that are not Daddy at all. Partners are frequently changed, and with sperm and egg donation and surrogate motherhood, the scale of confusion about our true identity is like an iceberg with a whole mountain of destruction under the surface.

Then there is the lack of meaning that many struggle with, a deep unfulfilled yearning where even if we are happy with our lives, we still feel overwhelmed with longings we don't even understand. How can we satisfy this ache? What does it even mean to be satisfied?

Maybe you've found yourself thinking: if only I had a body like that model, I would be happy; or, if my nose wasn't so big; if I had more money; a partner; a baby; drugs . . . The list is endless and can become all-consuming. We may develop a fixation on one particular desire with the result that drugs, sex, gambling, shopping or work become addictions covering up our deeper need to be loved unconditionally. But even the best of family love can never fill this void.

In addition to this universal need, we are faced with an epidemic migration from turmoil in the Middle East and the desperate needs of families broken by war. Even in our safe nations there is ongoing cultural change as we face terrorist threats and become home to the world's refugees. There is a colossal degree of insecurity everywhere.

But God is calling out to us: 'I love you, you are mine. You belong to me forever. I will never leave or forsake you. I died for you that you be totally loved, forgiven, pure and holy. I have chosen you to be my own beloved child. I take pleasure in you. You bring me so much joy. I delight in you. Come into that place of belonging with me, it is your right and your destiny to live with me and me with you. You are the apple of my eye.'

Pause and reflect

Reflect upon those words of love from your Father's heart. How do they make you feel? Don't cynically dismiss them if you cannot feel their truth as yet. You may need more healing if your emotions have been blocked off for a long time. But lack of feeling can never alter the truth of God's love and his affection for you. Look again at these verses in Ephesians 1:4,5:

> For he chose us in him before the creation of the world to be holy and blameless in his sight. In love he predestined us for adoption to sonship through Jesus Christ, in accordance with his pleasure and will.

'Chosen' is an amazingly healing word, and one that it could be very beneficial to spend time meditating upon in this passage, where it is surrounded by expressions of God's delight in us. Such love and delight are the truths that will make our foundation strong and stable.

As a child I associated the term 'chosen' with negatives. At school I was often chosen to be the subject of ridicule. Even some of the teachers would choose to make an example of me, picking me out in front of the class to shame me for not concentrating on what they were saying. I *was* concentrating, but what none of us knew was that I was deaf, as it wasn't fully diagnosed until I was 12, despite having become deaf when I was 2 through encephalitis. So when the teachers shouted in front of the class about how stupid I was, I believed them. I had no means of refuting their words, so what else could I be but stupid?

Similarly, when I was chosen after the age of 9 to be a target of verbal and sexual abuse, I had nothing with which to refute the things that were happening to me. So the experience of being chosen became full of shame and fear.

We can take such experiences into our reading of the Bible and view God's words of love as if we're looking at our reflections in a hall of mirrors. All those distortions that make us laughingly scream at ourselves and each other, knowing that the truth is very different, become much more sinister when we apply them to God's Word and character.

But in this passage God is saying he was thinking about us and chose us to belong to him, not just before we were born but before this world was formed. He anticipated us, planning when we would be born and to whom. Our minds are finite and we cannot grasp how God can love every one of us through the entire span of history. We say, 'I am just one of trillions, how can God know or care about me?' But Jesus said in Matthew 10:29–31:

> Are not two sparrows sold for a penny? Yet not one of them will fall to the ground outside your Father's care. And even the very hairs of your head are all numbered. So don't be afraid; you are worth more than many sparrows.

That same Father who counts the hairs on your head and watches over the life of every sparrow is saying to you: 'You may feel you are just one out of millions and therefore don't matter, but I tell you that you are *one in a million* and the apple of my eye.'

For reflection

Read this poem which I wrote while looking at the photo of a dear friend and her new baby and suddenly understanding what the spiritual term 'new birth' really means. It was a heart revelation that brought me deep healing, and I believe can do the same for you. Spend time talking to your heavenly Father about your reactions.

Mother and Child

I see the mother with her baby at her breast
Looking into his face with such tender love.
He is hers, she knows him.
Formed from her own body, her own genes,
Even her own blood supply.
Without her to sustain him, he could not have been,
He would have remained an idea, a seed.
But not become a child, a being in his own right.
Her blood, his blood, her nurture, his life.
She has emptied herself, been broken inside,
Willingly given up all she embraced within
Yet even as she was torn in two,
She gazed in adoration
Upon her newborn, her loved one, her child.
So too with my God.
He looks upon me with such tender love.
He knows me, for I am his.
He formed me in my mother's womb.
It was his hands that wove me together in the secret place.
He, the creator of this universe, stamped my DNA
With the kiss of his own image.
Through his precious blood poured out for me,
He re-birthed me; a new, true birth.
Without him to sustain me, I would have remained a shell,
A broken gift; a shattered dream.
But not become a daughter, a person in my own right.
The Spirit nurturing me into life.

For me, Jesus emptied himself,
Willingly forfeiting his Father's love.
Yet even as he was beaten, torn, crucified,
Even as he smashed forever the rocks of death
Even then, he gazed in adoration upon me,
His newborn.[3]

Believing and not doubting

In James 1:5–8 we see another important message about laying true foundations:

> If any of you lacks wisdom, you should ask God, who gives generously to all without finding fault, and it will be given to you. But when you ask, you must believe and not doubt, because the one who doubts is like a wave of the sea, blown and tossed by the wind. That person should not expect to receive anything from the Lord. Such a person is double-minded and unstable in all they do.

This rich passage reveals the Father's character and the importance of us living in partnership with him on a daily basis, so that as we come to him we know that he is good and desires to give to us. If that is our core belief, our prayers will be fuelled by a joyful trust. Jesus often exhibited such joy when he prayed, showing it so obviously that his disciples all noticed.

Conversely, if deep down we believe that God is not interested in answering our prayers, they become disempowered. As James describes so graphically, we can be like a 'wave of the sea, blown and tossed by the wind'. Waves are at the mercy of powerful forces like wind and tide. At one moment the sea may be calm, its waves gently lapping, but as soon as there's a strong breeze, they rise up and start hurling themselves in all directions.

Looking back at what James says, there are four main truths that we need to take hold of.

1. God delights in us asking him for what we need.
2. God gives generously.
3. God gives to *all*, not just a favoured few.
4. God chooses to not find fault with us.

In this illustration, James is talking about wisdom. Wisdom from God is something we need every day. It's not simply knowing what to do in certain situations, but is the essence of our partnership with him, hearing his voice and becoming like him in all our reactions.

But the fact that God loves to give to us all without finding fault applies to *everything*, not just wisdom. God our Father is a giving God. He delights to give to us and will give what is just right. He wants to be in partnership with us, and that means for us to have hearts of expectation every time we come to him.

Marilyn's story

At the beginning of 2015 Marilyn was preparing to go to Germany with a friend, Hilary, and they were due to leave at 2 p.m. But Marilyn couldn't find an important bank card that she needed. We searched everywhere to no avail and advised Marilyn to cancel the card. Marilyn knew this was sensible but her heart sank and she didn't know how she would manage without access to that account. She began to pray (she'd been praying in a flap, 'Lord, help me find that card!') but now she prayed in a different way, listening for his voice: 'Lord, what shall I do? Should I cancel my card?'

Much to her shock, a clear thought came back that she knew was from him: 'Don't cancel it, all is well.'

How could that be? She felt puzzled and quite anxious as by now there was only an hour to go. But she knew that voice and decided to follow it. She thought she might find the card immediately but no joy, so she gave up as she needed to finish packing. She was upstairs when I suddenly heard a commotion and she came running down full of amazement. She had been sorting out her technical gadgets and had dropped a tiny plug which rolled under the bed. Hilary pushed her hand under the bed to try to find it. She felt a hard edge alongside the plug and managed to draw it out. She was astonished to discover she was holding Marilyn's missing card! How incredible that Marilyn dropped the plug and Hilary put her hand under at just the point where the card lay hidden. Marilyn's bed is the type that comes right down to the floor so there's no way they could have seen it, and who would imagine a bank card being under a bed? But God knew and wanted to amaze Marilyn and fill her heart with joy, as well as enable her to find her lost card. It would have been such a waste to have cancelled it. So when she asked him, he gave her wisdom and told her it was OK. He didn't find fault and say, 'Well, you deserve to lose it, you should have taken more care!'

This is the kind of miracle God wants all of us to experience. He delights to engage with us in our everyday lives. Every time we experience something like this we can then choose to 'root' that experience in our hearts so that our foundations of trust get deeper and richer.

 Pause and reflect

- Returning at the end of this chapter to the concept of house building – if the buildings of our lives need the same strong foundations that real houses do, how can you ensure yours are healthy?
- If foundation stones had names, what names would you give those you are building into your life? Write them down in your journal.
- Like the cement that binds stones together to build a strong wall, truth is the vital ingredient that binds together all the essential stones of God's love. The *truth* of God's love for you, the *truth* of his Word, his character, his forgiveness; what he says about you.
- Write down some of the life-giving truths that you have learned throughout this chapter, and ask the Lord to use them to make you strong and secure.
- Read this very simple prayer written by David, and make it your own: 'Guide me in your truth and teach me, for you are God my Saviour, and my hope is in you all day long' (Ps. 25:5).

5

You Matter to Him

Did you know there's someone who can hear your faintest sigh? Someone who can hear your heart's deepest cry?

Marilyn Baker

Extract taken from the song 'He Gives Joy' by Marilyn Baker (Authentic). Copyright © 1982 Authentic Publishing.*

Your prayers matter

Recently I heard the story of a little girl with cerebral palsy called Sally who was staying at a Christian 'safe house' because of an abusive father. There were lots of other children there too and as it was summer they were enjoying riding around the large garden on the various bikes and scooters. The director, Lynn, who had been telling them how much Jesus loved them, was sitting with Sally on the grass. None of the bikes were suitable for her and Lynn could tell she felt sad.

'I'm sorry we haven't a bike for you, Sally,' Lynn said softly.

'Can we ask Jesus to get me one? You said he answers all our prayers,' Sally asked, snuggling into Lynn's side.

Lynn gulped; did she really believe that praying would bring them a suitable bike for a child with cerebral palsy? She didn't even know if there was such a thing.

'I'm going to ask Jesus to bring me one now!' shouted Sally, her arms jerking wildly as her excitement overflowed. 'Then I can play with the others and be the same as them!'

'Jesus, please do something,' Lynn prayed silently as Sally enthusiastically told Jesus what she wanted.

After lunch Lynn had a visitor, Jane, a lady who was a great prayer supporter of the work. They sat together looking into the gardens through the open patio doors. Many of the children were still playing outside as it was a beautiful day. Sally was outside too, sitting alone on the grass surrounded by dolls but ignoring them and looking wistfully at the other children as they played on their bikes.

'That poor child needs a bike,' said Jane, nodding towards Sally.

'She does,' Lynn agreed, and was just about to tell Jane how Sally had prayed when she realised Jane was still speaking.

'I know just the thing!' Jane exclaimed, jumping up. 'I have a friend whose disabled child has grown out of their special tricycle. She told me last week that she really hoped to find another child who could benefit from it. I will call and see if she still has it and if so, I'll go and get it straight away.' She got out her mobile and Lynn could tell from her excited response that it was good news. Jane put her phone down, beaming. 'She's still got it!' she cried, happily. 'I can go now to fetch it and she will wipe it all down and oil it so it goes well. She's so excited it will be going to a child who really needs it.'

Jane was about to rush off but Lynn stopped her. 'One moment,' she said, and she filled Jane in on Sally's prayer. When she finished, Jane was fizzing with excitement. 'That makes it even more wonderful, and will bless Sue so much!' she exclaimed. 'I'll come straight back, so look out for me later this afternoon. It'll be amazing to see Sally's face.'

She rushed off and Lynn continued with her jobs. Every time she saw Sally she longed to scoop her up and tell her the good news. Three hours later she was relieved to hear the doorbell. Excitedly she swung it open and saw Jane holding a brightly coloured, sturdy little tricycle. Lynn had worried it would look strange but it was much like any other trike, just with an extra wide seat and safety features. She breathed deeply, challenged by this small child's faith. Sally had already been through untold trauma in her short life with her disability and her violent father, but she'd simply taken on board that Jesus would answer her prayers.

Lynn and Jane hurried out of the house and came up behind Sally where she was sitting on the grass. 'Sally!' Lynn cried. 'Look what Jesus has brought you.'

Sally spun round and then with a shriek of joy reached out for the trike and pulled it towards her. Lynn moved to help but Sally was already struggling to her feet, using the trike for leverage. Quicker than Lynn had ever seen her move, she managed to climb into the seat. She was laughing and her arms flailed in her excitement. 'Jesus brought me my trike!' she shrieked, her face nearly splitting in two with her huge smile. Laughing with her, Lynn and Jane clicked the safety harness shut and helped Sally position her feet on the boxy pedals, wonderful for a child with such poor co-ordination. Amazingly, they were the perfect height and would need no adjustment. Lynn hadn't been sure if Sally would actually be able to pedal it, but they held her feet so securely that in moments she was moving along the path, gripping the handlebars just like any other child. Lynn felt a huge lump in her throat. This was all Sally's faith, she realised: 'I say that Jesus cares and will answer their prayers, but don't always believe it myself, but Sally just trusted, told Jesus what she wanted and it came.'

For the rest of the day it was one of the most joyful experiences Lynn had ever had, to sit with Jane watching Sally happily riding her new trike, with the other children egging her on. Now at last Sally was part of the group; she belonged.

Simple childlike trust

I love this story as it shows so powerfully that we matter to our Father and he loves to answer our prayers. The giving of that perfect trike on the very day Sally prayed is a wonderful example of the Father's kiss. He loves birthing joy in our hearts. Do you know that the things that matter to us also matter to him? Jesus teaches us this in Matthew 7:9–11, when he illustrates Father God's desire to give to us abundantly by pointing us to our desire to give to our own children:

> Which of you, if your son asks for bread, will give him a stone? Or if he asks for a fish, will give him a snake? If you, then, though you are evil, know how to give good gifts to your children, how much more will your Father in heaven give good gifts to those who ask him!

Giving to our children is part of being a good parent. And that comes from us all being made in God's image. If it is natural to give to our own children, this must come from God whose very nature is to give; he does so with no ulterior motives, so his gifts are always perfect. He knows exactly what we need and how we will be most blessed. We only see our lives with finite vision so sometimes our prayers flow out of anxiety or cultural pressure rather than out of the joy of being God's child. So God's answer to our prayers may at times be different to what we asked for, or he may want us to wait, for the time is not yet right. But he always hears and wants to bless us.

Similarly, we may not give our children exactly what they ask for because of the cost or danger. Would you give your 5-year-old son a motorbike? But you may give him something much more appropriate to his age, like a scooter.

Jesus gave this illustration because he wants us to know that we matter to God and that he hears everything that is on our hearts. I feel sometimes that God won't answer my prayers because I haven't been very good, or because he is so glorious, my tiny needs won't matter. But Jesus is telling us that as God's beloved children our needs matter 100 per cent.

As a blind person, Marilyn can easily lose things, especially tiny things like earrings. She tells the story of how when she was young she dropped something and prayed God would help her find it as she'd heard a sermon on the radio about God helping us even when we lose things. Her mum heard her and laughed, saying that God was very busy and had far more important things to think about. Marilyn was disappointed, feeling she'd been silly, but after becoming a Christian began to realise that all our concerns matter to him. Years later her earring and its butterfly flew out of her hand and landed in different places on the carpet. She began to feel in the thick pile, praying the Lord would help her, as the earrings were a gift from a close friend who had since died. Amazingly, she found the earring itself immediately but no sign of the butterfly. She prayed again, thanking him that he knew where it was. She felt she should search around the other side of her bed which seemed unlikely, but she did and straight away felt the tiny metal butterfly. How wonderful! She was full of thankfulness, and still has those earrings today.

 **Pause and reflect**

Read these verses from Psalm 34:15:

> The eyes of the LORD are on the righteous, and his ears are attentive to their cry.

> The Lord sees all we do; he watches over his friends day and night. His godly ones receive the answers they seek whenever they cry out to him. (TPT)

- When you think of the Lord 'seeing' and 'watching over' you, how does that make you feel?
- What do you imagine is in his heart as he watches you?
- What does the word 'attentive' in the NIV version tell you about his character?
- *The Passion Translation* describes him as giving the answers that his godly ones are seeking him for . . .
- How much and how expectantly are you seeking him and crying out to him for your needs, both big and small? Answer honestly, as there is no point in giving an 'expected' answer if it's not true for you.
- If your answer was positive, thank him for his attentive love and care for all your needs.
- If your answer was more hesitant and you know you find it hard to believe he cares, tell him this and ask him to help you.

A personal illustration

As I am partially sighted, I need my glasses to see to get around. However, they're not so good for reading, as they can make close-up things blurry. So I take them off but then lose them!

Some time ago we were going away, but I couldn't find my glasses. I searched everywhere and was getting desperate as we soon needed to leave. How could I travel without them?

So I prayed: 'Father, please help me find my glasses.'

A little later, as I passed our van to take some rubbish out, a clear thought came: 'Look in the van.'

'Why do that?' I thought. 'We haven't travelled for several days.' I dismissed it but the thought came again, more urgently. I was getting to know the voice of God, so although it seemed mad, I did open the passenger section of the van. I was sure I'd find the glasses but there was no sign of them, and I felt a gullible fool. 'God has got more important things to do than look after your glasses; you should have been more careful!' I scolded myself.

But as I continued searching, the thought came again, 'Look in the van.' I felt a bit exasperated. 'Lord, I've looked in the van already!'

'Look in the van.'

I sighed; the only other possible area was the back where we keep all our equipment. I swung the doors open and gazed at the keyboards and speakers. How could my glasses be here? In a lacklustre way I moved two crates slightly apart, and gasped. There in the crack were my glasses. It was only as I happily returned into the house that I remembered: that morning I'd been sorting our bookstall stock in the van for the coming events and must have removed my glasses to read something. I'd forgotten, but God certainly hadn't and when I sought him in desperation, he nudged me to look in the van.

You are loved to the same degree as Jesus

Jesus said to his disciples in John 15:9:

As the Father has loved me, so have I loved you. Now remain in my love.

A key word in this sentence is that tiny word 'as'. Do you realise this means you are loved to the same degree *as* Jesus?

Take a moment to reflect – you are loved just much as Jesus.

Here are just some of the things this may mean:

- you are loved as a son or a daughter
- you are chosen
- you are delighted in
- you please your heavenly Father
- you bring him joy
- you are accepted
- you have been made as clean and holy as Jesus
- your Father loves talking with you
- he loves listening to you
- he loves answering your prayers
- you are loved unconditionally
- he trusts and honours you

How does that make you feel? I find it mind-boggling even though I'm the one that's writing it. Take some time to go through the list and think about those phrases describing how he loves you.

Have you experienced him showing you his love in any of these ways?

What happened?

How did you feel?

How did it affect your faith?

Thank him for all the ways he's shown you his love, and write about them in your journal to treasure at a later time.

A healing dream revealing how we matter to him

The following dream was shared with me by a dear friend called Sharon. Her life circumstances constantly robbed her of self-esteem and it was hard for her to connect with a God of love. One night she dreamt she was blind. This probably sprang out of her feelings of isolation and lack of acceptance. In her own words:

> In the dream my friend invited me to a dance. I was reluctant to go but she was persistent. As the time approached I felt very nervous. My friends picked me up and on arrival we were shown our seats. As we ordered our meal I felt more relaxed, but after that my friends one by one excused themselves, saying, 'Do you mind if I go and dance?' I said, 'No, enjoy it.' They found partners and were soon dancing. I sat listening to the chit chat all around, feeling completely exposed for I am blind.
>
> Suddenly I felt a hand on my shoulder, and a softly spoken voice said, 'May I have the pleasure of this dance?'
>
> 'But,' I said, 'how can I dance? I am blind.'
>
> He said, 'I know.'
>
> He held my hand, and led me to the dance floor, saying, 'Put your hands on my arms and follow my movements.'
>
> As the music played, he led me around. I relaxed and rested my head on his shoulder and felt full of peace in his embrace. Then he said, 'I am your loving heavenly Father. I am always this close to you so never fear.' And he held me tight in his embrace all the time as I followed his movements. The dance was swift and beautiful. At the end my Father kissed me on the forehead and I knew he had sealed me in his love.[1]

This is for you too

This beautiful dream was for Sharon but as with all the prophetic gifts, the truth it expresses that God cares for us as his beloved children, is something we can all cherish. He was communicating to Sharon that she mattered and that he was with her in her isolation. As a Father he knew both her love of dance and the many wounds of rejection she carried, and he wanted to show her that she was held safely in his love, so he wove all these strands together into a dream.

Paul tells us in 1 Corinthians 14:1–3:

> Follow the way of love and eagerly desire gifts of the Spirit, especially prophecy . . . the one who prophesies speaks to people for their strengthening, encouraging and comfort.

A dream or vision like Sharon's comes under the umbrella of prophecy. It's all to do with seeing into heavenly dimensions and understanding things that humanly are not evident. As this verse indicates, prophecies are often given to encourage and comfort others who need his touch. But equally, we can seek him to reveal his heart to us for our own healing and comfort and this was what happened with Sharon.

A prophetic vision for someone

As I was writing, a vision came to me for someone reading this. I saw you as a small girl, maybe about 6 years old. You are cuddling a large, pretty doll and wanting it with you all the time as she helps you to feel safe. Because she is so big you hide behind her at difficult times and pretend no one can see you. But then I saw an unkind hand take the doll away and you are left on your own with nothing to protect you. You feel devastated, helpless and abandoned. Then I saw the Lord come and pick you up. He held you in his arms and the sleeves of his robe flowed over you, hiding you. He is so big that everything else is miniscule in comparison, including the owner of the big unkind hand who is now smaller than the Lord's toes. When you see how tiny he is in comparison to the Lord you sit up in the Lord's arms and laugh at him, and as you laugh the Lord laughs with you, and suddenly I see that you are changing from being a small girl into a strong and beautiful woman.

 **Pause and reflect**

This is a powerful picture that could help bring you real healing. It is revealing a traumatic time in your childhood where, with no one to turn to, you tried making a doll your protector. But when that doll was torn away, you felt exposed and helpless. I believe that part of you has always remained that frightened little girl, but God has come to heal that wound and enable you to become the beautiful woman you really are. I loved how the Lord's robes covered you, providing a hiding place where no one could see you. Secondly, I loved the humour of that unkind person now being smaller than the Lord's toes. It was awesome to see you sitting and laughing and the Lord laughing with you at the one who had imprisoned you in fear for so long. Your laughter freed you to grow into the strong and beautiful woman you are. This is a key for you, that out of intimacy with your Father, you will know laughter which will free you from every childhood trauma; for 'the joy of the LORD is your strength' (Neh. 8:10).

If this vision and interpretation have touched you, find a quiet place to enjoy some time with the Lord. Ask him to show you any specific memories that need healing. Allow his love to fill you. You are safe in his arms. If you feel it will help you, consider having some prayer ministry or counselling with someone you can trust.

Whose voice are you listening to?

Do you ever feel that those around you are more acceptable than you are? Maybe people care about you, but deep within a voice keeps saying: 'You don't matter, no one really loves you. What you do in your life doesn't interest anyone else.'

This voice is so insidious, whispering its negative lies and misrepresentations of the truth, and we can easily become ensnared by it. Sometimes I struggle in social situations because of my deafness. I chip in only to be met by blank looks. Embarrassed, I fumble to a stop, feeling at best, a fool and at worst, a failure. Then that whisper has a field day reminding me that I've got nothing interesting to add to the most ordinary of conversations. I know in my head that the voice is really Satan, but it's all too easy to believe. Unfortunately I don't have any problems hearing this negative, soul-destroying voice. It speaks all too clearly and takes hardly any time to send me on a negative, downward spiral that is crippling in its effects. This can happen even with close family members or friends. I might feel, for example, that because I can't chat with my mum as easily as my sister does, that I am not so lovable. But that's a lie. My mum may feel more at ease with my sister, as they have more in common and don't have the communication difficulties that I do, but that doesn't mean I am less lovable.

False Evidence Appearing Real (FEAR)

There is an acronym that Marilyn uses, made from, and describing, the word FEAR: 'False Evidence Appearing Real'. This is what that voice is. It seems easy to believe because it comes to us in the guise of being true. This is the 'evidence' that we're stupid, lazy, unwanted, a failure . . . it lays that so-called evidence before us and we believe it. Fear fills our hearts and we feel destined to fail.

But this voice is a mirage. It is not God's truth about us, but when we believe it, we open our hearts to the fear that the false evidence travels upon. We must realise that the evidence is not true and the fear is nothing in itself. Fear is one of Satan's primary strategies, but God says in Romans 8:14,15:

> For those who are led by the Spirit of God are the children of God. The Spirit you received does not make you slaves, so that you live in fear again; rather, the Spirit you received brought about your adoption to sonship. And by him we cry, '*Abba*, Father.'

God loves us unconditionally. We cannot fathom it as sadly the only love many of us have known has been conditional. Your parents may say they love you but you constantly feel that if you fail academically, have the wrong friends, or do the wrong things, then you won't be loved. Maybe you felt you'd be more loved if you were a boy/girl, or if you didn't have a particular disability?

Marilyn's father was devastated when she became blind shortly after birth. Her mum was able to walk through her grief and loved Marilyn as much as if she'd been a sighted child. But her dad became bitter and as Marilyn grew up, was completely unable to praise her, despite the fact that she excelled in music from a young age. His only comment on her school reports was always: 'You could have done better.' As I mentioned earlier, he repeatedly told her that she would be a nuisance to people if she asked for help. He spoke with a bitter authority that was impossible for Marilyn to just shrug off. She experienced a great deal of healing and transformation over the years, but deep inside these lies were still wounding her, and she found it difficult to ask for help without the pervading feeling that people would find her a nuisance.

Eventually a deeper healing began when Marilyn was on a retreat with the Christian writer Joyce Huggett. Joyce discerned from the Holy Spirit that Marilyn had, in effect, been worshipping a false picture of God because of this wound from her father. She led Marilyn to turn to the true Father who, as depicted by Jesus in the prodigal son story, was passionate about expressing his love and affection even when his son had messed up. Joyce felt that Marilyn needed to trust that Father God was similarly lavishing his affection on her. This is vital for us all.

So what are you rehearsing?

> The son said to him, 'Father, I have sinned against heaven and against you. I am no longer worthy to be called your son.'
>
> But the father said to his servants, 'Quick! Bring the best robe and put it on him' (Luke 15:21,22).

The son was so busy mentally rehearsing his own unworthiness that he failed to notice his dad running with his robes hitched up and his arms outstretched to embrace him. All the son could see was how he had failed. But all the dad could see was his long-lost son. The son spoke out rehearsed statements springing from condemnation, rather than true confession arising from conviction of sin which then leads to the peace of forgiveness. As Paul teaches in Romans 8:1,31–34:

> Therefore, there is now no condemnation for those who are in Christ Jesus . . . If God is for us, who can be against us? . . . Who will bring any charge against those whom God has chosen? It is God who justifies. Who then is the one who condemns?

Because of Jesus, God's forgiveness of us is absolute. There literally is nothing for us to be condemned about. God is for us. He is for *you*. He loved you so much he gave his precious son for you. Just as the father welcomed home his disaster of a son with a kiss that said, 'I love you son, you belong to me. I delight in you, I am proud of you', so God runs to embrace you.

Maybe you too have been rehearsing your own condemnation and have become blind to the loving presence of Father God running to embrace you? Do you try to cover all the bases with your confessions so that if he rejects you it won't hurt so much? Are the words you speak out or the thoughts you think full of peace, or condemnation?

Take hold of his peace today and know you are loved.

A story

Today I heard an amazing story showing that God is always with us and seeking to turn our lives around, even when we don't know him.

A friend of ours runs a ministry reaching out to people in crisis. She told us how a lady was in terrible financial debt and had no way to pay it. She became suicidal as she had young children and didn't know how she was going to continue looking after them. She was walking up the road in a daze when she suddenly found herself at a standstill outside a large bungalow that she'd never seen before. Nothing was in her way, but she couldn't move or stop staring at this house, and even began to feel compelled to knock at the door. It seemed crazy as she had no idea who lived there, but the urge grew stronger and she still couldn't move. Eventually she did knock and our friend answered and asked what she could do for her. The lady poured out her anguish, and our friend listened with real compassion and told her that it was God who had stopped her. The lady was amazed to think that God would be interested in her and for the first time began to feel some hope. Through trusted contacts, our friend was able to put her situation before the council, and in an incredibly short time, the lady had received help and was able to start putting her life together again.

I love this story as it demonstrates so well how interested the Lord is in every detail of our lives. It reminds me of the story in Acts 10 where the Holy Spirit speaks to Cornelius and tells him to send men to Joppa to find Peter:

> At Caesarea there was a man named Cornelius, a centurion in what was known as the Italian Regiment . . . One day at about three in the afternoon he had a vision. He distinctly saw an angel of God, who came to him and said, 'Cornelius!' Cornelius stared at him in fear. 'What is it, Lord?' he asked. The angel answered . . . 'Now send men to Joppa to bring back a man named Simon who is called Peter. He is staying with Simon the tanner, whose house is by the sea.' . . . About noon the following day as they were on their journey and approaching the city, Peter went up on the roof to pray (vv. 1–9).

Peter then had three visions about the unclean animals being let down in the sheet and the voice of God telling him to kill and eat. This was totally contrary to Peter's beliefs so the Holy Spirit needed to show him three times. He didn't understand it, just as that lady who felt compelled to go and knock on the door had no understanding of what was happening. But the Father knew how to reach her, and also knew how to communicate a deeper understanding to Peter. Anointed timing that is clearly engineered by the Holy Spirit is one of God's love strategies to grab our attention and enable us to see that he is in control in our lives.

While Peter was wondering about the meaning of the vision, the men sent by Cornelius found out where Simon's house was and stopped at the gate. They called out, asking if Simon who was known as Peter was staying there ... the Spirit said to him, 'Simon, three men are looking for you. So get up and go downstairs. Do not hesitate to go with them, for I have sent them' (vv. 19,20).

Isn't it awesome how all the details of this divine encounter were worked out? This is the Father's great love for all. He will never confine himself to just a chosen few, for his passion is for all to come to know him. How wonderful that he took note of details like the fact that Peter was hungry, for the vision was tapping into that natural sensation of hunger. How wonderful that he spoke to Cornelius so that his men travelled to Joppa, arriving just in time for Peter to be spiritually ready because of the vision he'd just received. Here's what happened as a result: Peter is at the house of Cornelius and has been sharing about Jesus ...

While Peter was still speaking these words, the Holy Spirit came on all who heard the message. The circumcised believers who had come with Peter were astonished that the gift of the Holy Spirit had been poured out even on Gentiles. For they heard them speaking in tongues and praising God. Then Peter said, 'Surely no one can stand in the way of their being baptised with water. They have received the Holy Spirit just as we have' (vv. 44–47).

Just as that suicidal woman mattered so much to God that he stopped her from progressing further up the road until she'd visited the bungalow, and just as Cornelius and his family mattered so much that God arranged all the details of their encounter with Peter, so do you matter to him. Every detail of your life is known to him. Every prayer you pray, every cry of your heart is heard. He loves you and has taken away everything that would stop you being able to enjoy his love. You are his beloved child.

A God-given picture and prophecy for you

As I write I can sense his overwhelming love for someone. You feel a deep shame about yourself as if you are saying in your heart, 'I am disgusting, I'm only worthy to be thrown into the bin, just like dogs' mess is picked up and thrown away.'

I feel God's deep sorrow for you and longing to show you that he has blotted out all the shame you are carrying. In a picture I see you standing before him and you will not meet his eyes. You look down, and as I follow your gaze I see you are wearing a filthy robe. It is covered with shaming, demeaning words. You believe these words are the truth of who you are and that nothing can alter that. But he calls out to you: 'Come to me out of the clefts of the rock, out of your hiding place of shame. Please stop hiding your face as it is so beautiful to me. I want to see you and be with you. I want to enjoy time with you and treasure your company. I want to hear you, because all that you say or even think is beautiful to me' (Song 2:14, paraphrased).

He embraces you, pulling you close so your head is nestled against his chest. You are startled as you hear his heart beating. You feel safe but you 'know' you have no right to be there. Suddenly he starts laughing, a great joyous laugh, and you are shocked, but as you look up into his face you see that he is also weeping, with tears pouring down his chest. You gasp as this river of tears cascades over every part of your being. Suddenly you hear him speaking and his very voice is like the sound of many waters (Rev. 1:15): 'Beloved child, I love you and am for you. You are mine. Who can condemn you? You are white, clean and beautiful before me. I've washed you and made you new. You are utterly pure.'

You feel such a longing for these words to be true, but even as he speaks you hear an opposing voice: 'He must be blind if he thinks I am pure. I am filthy.'

But he simply says: 'Look at yourself, child. See the truth of what I have done for you.' And you follow his gaze and see that your very robe has now become a pure, unblemished white. All the disgusting words are gone. It is dazzling and fits you perfectly and you realise it could be for no one else. It is your own robe, your own being. You lift up your head and bask in the river of his tears and know all your shame and ugliness have truly been washed away. He laughs again and as you experience him expressing such joy over you, his laughter penetrates to the depths of your being and for the first time ever you feel an explosion of joy bursting within you.

 Pause and reflect

- Take a while to reflect on this holy picture/prophecy. Thank him that he has truly washed you clean and lovingly removed all condemnation.
- The robe in the picture was covered with negative and shaming words. Ask the Lord to reveal any lies of condemnation that you've believed and so given Satan power to keep tormenting you through. For example, 'You're a failure.'
- Thank him for all he did for you on the cross and that you are totally forgiven, and that therefore these lies are null and void.
- Read Zechariah 3:1–5 and Zephaniah 3:14,15 and 17 and thank and praise him that this is his heart for you.
- Spend time basking in his love.

6

Noticing the Father's Presence

Here I am! I stand at the door and knock. If anyone hears my voice and opens the door, I will come in and eat with that person, and they with me.

Rev. 3:20

Jesus tells us that he is knocking at the door of our lives, hoping we will invite him in. How amazing that the One who made this whole universe would ask for our permission to enter the secret place of our hearts. I love the intimacy that this implies. He wants us to eat and relax together. Sharing meals and growing in friendship with one another is something that spans all religions, cultures and ages. It's a picture of togetherness and celebration. God wants us to enjoy that with him too. He is not absent, working in some distant sphere and just tolerating an occasional reminder of our existence. Rather, this is a God whose greatest desire is to be with us.

Jesus said, 'if anyone hears my voice and opens the door . . . '

He's not just knocking but calling too, longing for us to hear his voice. As a deaf person I can miss doorbells and fail to follow a conversation. But when I do connect with someone and we laugh or cry together and know we've both been heard, I find it exhilarating.

This is the kind of happiness we are all invited to enter into with Jesus. We will need to practise and mature in listening to him, but he has given us all we need to hear his voice. The only thing that may stop us is our own unbelief or hardness of heart. Maybe you believe he has saved you but still keep your guard up to any real intimacy with him? That inner guardedness is the door he is lovingly calling you to open. He said, 'Here I am!' He is here in the present moment, not some far-off time. He's not going to abandon us.

In Matthew 28:20, he makes that very clear, saying: 'Surely I am with you always, to the very end of the age.'

Immanuel, God is with us

So what does it mean that God is with us always? At Christmas I send out cards saying: ' . . . a virgin shall conceive and bear a son, and shall call his name Immanuel [God with us]' (Isa. 7:14 AMPC).

Immanuel, God is with us. Is this a reality to you? I love the promise of peace and security it contains. I can be at rest because my God is with me. I am safe because Jesus is at my side. I will never be alone because he has chosen me to belong to him forever. He is close to me and has called me to be close to him. It is a relationship of trust, joy and power, because his love is real.

Recently I experienced what being at rest in his presence can mean. I was staying at a little conference centre with a group of deaf friends for the Open Ears (Hard of Hearing Christian Fellowship) annual break. Breakfast was served at 8 a.m. followed immediately by a session. I had my hearing dog, Goldie, with me and needed to take him out at 7 a.m., as there would be no time after breakfast. The problem was that at 7 a.m. it was pitch dark. My sight is worse in the dark so, on the first morning, I gingerly stepped out the door and made my way carefully along the path. Goldie had already disappeared and I could hear him foraging amongst the autumn leaves. I was already struggling to see and hadn't yet left the lit path. I reached the turn to the woods and hesitantly shuffled forward. It was so dark that I couldn't tell where the trees were, although I remembered from my daytime walk that there was a large horse chestnut somewhere in front of me. The ground was uneven and criss-crossed by tree roots. I felt I'd never successfully manage the walk without tripping.

'Lord, please help me,' I prayed.

I suddenly had a clear awareness of his answer: 'Child, I am with you, relax.' Peace filled me. I still couldn't see but I knew in a way I hadn't before that he would keep me safe. I sensed him encouraging me to walk as freely as if I could actually see. This seemed crazy but I tried. I'd been quite tensed up through nervousness but I relaxed and began to saunter along. There was only a very rough track and that was completely invisible, but somehow my feet stayed level and on the few occasions when there was a root I somehow knew as I put my foot down and was able to step over it safely. I felt that the Lord and I were on an adventure together and he was protecting and guiding me. I began to hear the sounds of the woods, the rustle of the leaves, and the crackle of twigs and foliage underfoot. When I am relaxed I can still sometimes hear these sounds but generally I lose them, as they get absorbed into the racket of unclassified noise that is my deafness. When I suddenly heard the pure song of a bird welcoming the dawn I felt such joy. It seemed the Lord had arranged it specially that I would be in the woods at just the right time and helped me to relax with the amazing result of me hearing this beautiful song.

But a short while later, a thorny branch got caught in my hair and abruptly stopped me. While struggling to disentangle myself I stepped sideways and my feet started sliding down what felt like a bank. The earth was taking on a distinctly sticky feel. Alarmed that I was about to fall into a stream (as indeed it turned out to be), I scrambled wildly, just managing to stop myself from falling in and also freeing myself from the branch. I was safe but felt rather cross.

'Lord, you told me to relax as you would guide and keep me safe, but I've nearly fallen into a stream and lost half my hair. That was exactly the kind of thing I was worried would happen,' I berated him.

'But you didn't fall, did you? And don't you think you're exaggerating a bit to say you lost half your hair? Remember, I know exactly how many hairs you have and to my knowledge you only lost one and that was due to be replaced today anyway! Also I have a message I want to give someone through you being safe despite walking into the branch and nearly stepping into the stream, so listen to me, child . . . '

I couldn't believe that God would use my own silliness in going for a walk in the dark to speak prophetically, but I listened and in the stillness he dropped a tender message of love and care into my heart for someone else in the group. This is the essence of what it was. Maybe it will speak to you too? At the time when I shared it, a lady in her eighties responded and was deeply touched by the Lord as a result.

> Beloved child, I am with you. I know how anxious you have become in life and how you feel afraid that you cannot see what is ahead. You are fearful of getting entangled in negative situations, so fearful that you refrain from becoming involved in anything in case it affects you. You fear making mistakes or feeling out of your depth. You were hurt and now your fear and expectation of difficulties are more real to you than me and the security I offer you. Let me take that fear, beloved child. I have good plans for you, plans to give you a hope and a future. I am always with you to protect and guide you. Don't let the enemy imprison you to the past but put your hand in mine and walk forward with expectation. And I will bring you out into a new place, a spacious place of joy and wonder.

Pause and reflect

- Spend a while thinking about my story and this prophetic message.
- Are there areas of your life where you hold back out of fear?
- Can you talk to him about them?
- When I was fearful of walking in the dark, he told me to walk as confidently as if I could see. He wanted to take away my fear by encouraging me to step out in trust. Listen to him for any ideas he may give you for overcoming your own fear.
- What does his promise that he is always with you mean to you?
- Can you joyfully accept that he has good plans for you?

A story of Father's voice

Just as God spoke to me on that walk, he wants to speak to you, to give you revelation, comfort and insight to help others too. Have you heard him today? He will speak to us in many ways, so it's important we make time to listen and enter that secret place of intimacy that Jesus gave us access to. This doesn't just mean in spiritual mountain-top experiences but in the midst of great struggles too. Sometimes life can be very tough. Can we really experience his help and comfort in those times? Do we even listen to God when life hits us in the face? The following testimony was shared by a friend who'd had a good childhood, was close to her parents and happily working as a doctor, and then, in her own words:

Something terrible happened – suddenly my world turned upside down. My mother was killed in a road accident. I was in the back of the car and every minute of that night is stored in my head, outlined in black felt-tip pen, colours vibrant and bright, lights flashing, every sound echoing. I can recall exactly the feel of her coat in my hand as I tried to rouse her, leaning forward through the back of the car, my hand on her shoulder: 'Mum? Mum?'

Many things were said to comfort me in the days that followed. 'All things work to good' was said in church one day when I was tearful. 'It'll make you a better doctor in the end.' (All true of course but completely bad timing.)

But where was God? How could he have let this happen? My brother had prayed before we left that we would have a safe journey. And we hadn't. Why, why? I wasn't that bad a person; I didn't deserve this agonising, gut-churning pain. I thought I would never smile again. I was angry with God. I couldn't speak to him or pray. I wanted him but didn't want him. I needed his love but couldn't string a prayer together.

So what happened next? It wasn't really until some years later that I realised I was responding like a toddler with my hands over my ears singing 'la la la' so as not to hear my parents calling me.

God had to shout to get my attention, and shout he did. I began to experience him in ways I never had before. He jumped out from pages of books, TV programmes, things I saw and in dreams and visions. Some things I barely registered, but one I couldn't deny and it was a turning point in my grieving. God gave me a vision. I was walking around in heaven. There were tall white buildings. The sky was azure blue (like the sky of my childhood) and there was beautiful music. I saw many people all dressed in beautiful white robes and there was contentment and a deep happiness. I could not see her, but I knew with certainty that my mother was there. Then I heard God ask me if I really wanted my mother to leave heaven and return to the dirt and grime of earth? Of course I knew I didn't. So from that point, I did actually stop wishing her back again, not that I missed her any the less. So that was my experience of my Father's care – shouting at me when I had my hands over my ears.

Grieving is a long process and I have never stopped learning.[1]

 Pause and reflect

- Does Wendy's experience gel with you in any way?
- What was wrong with the comments people made in the face of her grief?
- Wendy said God was shouting to get her attention even when she was not listening. What does this tell you about his love?
- How did God speak to her in the end? Have you experienced his voice through such channels?
- What was the fruit of God's message as opposed to listening to people's attempts to comfort?
- Talk to him about your responses.

Pictures of God's goodness from our earthly dads

Many of us had difficult experiences with our earthly parents and, tragically, the impact has been shattering. Violent dads can completely destroy a growing child's trust and so can the experience of the lack of a father figure, the feeling of not mattering because work is more important, or he leaves for another woman . . . An older lady we met once had major problems with her abusive mother, but one of her deepest griefs was that her dad had been too weak to withstand his wife's violent temper. He didn't protect his children at all and this completely eradicated any trust she might have had in God's fatherly protection. Another lady had parents who were highly overprotective, not just of their daughter but of the family reputation too. She was forbidden to do anything that incurred risk or would bring them public attention. She grew up fearful of stepping out of line or letting them down, which in turn caused a debilitating anxiety syndrome. Her father loved her but his own fears impacted his treatment of her, causing his love to become a form of control rather than the unconditional acceptance that it always is from God.

Personally, I have very few memories of my dad apart from my prevailing memory of the months when he was in hospital when he was very ill with cancer. I remember visiting him and feeling overwhelmed with the strangeness of seeing him in this environment. Once he returned home to die, it was even harder. Why was Daddy sleeping in the lounge? Why was he coughing all the time? Why didn't he ever get up? I remember my sister, who was three years older, sitting for hours at his bedside, chatting and doing her homework there, fetching things for him and generally loving being with him. I would stand in the doorway watching, but don't remember being with him in the same way. I am sure my mum was protecting me as I was younger and more fragile because of my illness. But while I may understand now, as children we cannot rationalise things. All I knew was that I felt disconnected. I have few memories of my dad cuddling, playing games, or spending time with me. Recently, I asked my mum what he was like and said I couldn't really remember him, and she pointed out that because he too had been made deaf through encephalitis (in his case when he was 22), he didn't find socialising easy and may have struggled to know how to communicate with me.

So as I had a real gulf in my understanding of what it means to be fathered, I asked some friends to tell me their good memories of how their dads showed their affection. I found some of their responses very moving.

'My dad has always been someone I could turn to and he always had open arms to hold me and an open heart to listen. He's a very special man to me' – G.T.

'If I was really upset and he tried to hug me I'd fight it but he wouldn't budge and would just hold me tighter until I relaxed and give into the healing tears then he'd talk to me and everything would be OK' – J.W.

'He worked hard to ensure his family had all they needed and was not only generous with material things but most importantly his love and his time' – P.M.

'My dad in his last week coming to put his arm around my shoulders when I was washing up and I was crying' – M.G.

'Sitting safely on Dad's knee as he reads to me from the children's Bible ... sitting in his shed watching him working' – L.C.

'My dad was very special. Although low income, we had holidays while he stayed behind to work ... He managed to find enough money to buy special cakes when my pen-friend came to stay. When he had to go into a care home the carers went into his room all the time as his beaming smile always cheered them up' – S.G.

'My dad has a great sense of humour. As kids I remember lots of lovely trips to the seaside and funfair. He would ride the big dipper with us. Friday nights he would bring us sweeties. He gave us a very happy childhood' – L.T.

'I remember my lovely dad as always being there for us' – C.S.

'Unconditional love, a feeling of safety. A very honest, trustworthy, gentle man. He loved his family, worked long hours to provide for us all and still found time to play with my brother and I when he came home' – A.M.

'My dad adopted me as his own. He's the only father I have ever known and he's my hero' – R.V.

Beautiful reflection of God's Father heart

All these glimpses into our earthly experiences of fatherhood also reveal glimpses of our heavenly Father's heart of love. Genesis 1:26,27 says that we were made in God's image:

> Then God said, 'Let us make mankind in our image, in our likeness, so that they may rule over the fish in the sea and the birds in the sky, over the livestock and all the wild animals . . . ' So God created mankind in his own image, in the image of God he created them; male and female he created them.

Part of God's plan in making us in his image was that we would demonstrate to our children his parental heart. He is the ultimate Father and Mother. What we have cherished from our own mums and dads, he gives to us in much greater measure. So if our earthly fathers have gone out of their way to provide for us and make sure all our material needs are met, that is just a fraction of the way our heavenly Father loves to meet our needs. If our earthly fathers have comforted us when we are sad, how much more does our heavenly Father love to comfort and help us to mature during times of struggle? Listen to this description of his character in 2 Corinthians 1:3,4:

> Praise be to the God and Father of our Lord Jesus Christ, the Father of compassion and the God of all comfort, who comforts us in all our troubles, so that we can comfort those in any trouble with the comfort we ourselves receive from God.

He is the Father of compassion and the God of all comfort. If we have known comfort and compassion from our own dads, then that comes from our Father God in whose image we have all been made. Conversely, if we have only known wounding from our mums and dads, this is *not* God's heart for us and he longs to come to us in our brokenness and heal our wounds and wrap us in his compassion. We need to open our hearts to see how God might be showing us his love.

Pause and reflect

- Read back over those quotations of good father experiences.
- Can you add your own good memories, or have you never experienced hands-on father/mother love?
- Talk to your heavenly Father about your memories and feelings. If you have happy memories, thank him and ask him to open your heart to his even greater Father love.
- If your memories are painful, remember he is *not* a father who wounds you in any way but *is* the Father of all comfort and compassion. Give him your hurt and ask him to help you to know him as your true loving Father.
- Write in your journal what you have just prayed.

Quality focus

If I am spending quality time with someone, listening, sharing, having fun together, I can't give anyone else my attention in the same way at the same time. I may be chatting with others, but it won't be that in-depth attention that I am writing of here. When I am focusing on the one, someone may give me a message but it will be a momentary interruption. I will then turn back to the first one. This is true for us all, although some are better at focusing on more people at once, for example, if we have young children. But even then there is a limit and we can find ourselves getting 'thinly spread' in our ability to give everyone what they need. Sometimes we think God struggles in the same way, but he is different. Each one of us is his number one. Every hair on our head is counted. Every sparrow that falls to the ground is known and loved by him.

In the midst of our everyday, the chaos of bringing up small children or of caring for an elderly parent; the rush of fulfilling our job requirements, cleaning our homes, gardening, keeping up with church, friends and family, he tells us in John 14:18:

> I will not leave you as orphans; I will come to you.

He is there with you when everything is a struggle and you can hardly face the day. He is equally there with you when you jump out of bed full of enthusiasm. He weeps when you weep and rejoices when you rejoice. When you are over-busy and stop making time for him, he is there, wanting to help you and give you his peace.

Letting him help

I remember once feeling very frazzled as we had visitors coming to stay but we'd had a busy day with no opportunity to prepare. I still had all the bedrooms to clean and beds to make up. The clock was edging nearer to teatime when the Lord dropped a thought in my heart: 'Why don't you let me help you?'

I felt a bit exasperated. 'Lord, how can you help, I can hardly give you the hoover!'

'I am with you.'

'Yes, I know you're with me, Lord, and I thank you, but I have all these jobs to do!'

'Just ask me, child. Everything that matters to you matters to me, and if I say I will help you, I will.'

I knew when I was beaten. 'OK, Lord, thank you that you are with me. Please help me to get everything ready so that I can be relaxed when the visitors arrive instead of in a tizz.'

I didn't know what to expect . . . certainly not that he would dust the shelves. But suddenly I felt a real peace enter my spirit. It was as if in some deep way I was able to let go of the need to have everything perfect. I started to worship him and joy filled my heart. Amazingly, all the jobs were accomplished with ease, even the dinner was cooking nicely when the visitors knocked a couple of hours later. I was full of joy that my Father had indeed helped me in ways that I would never have expected, and which turned out to be much more worthwhile than simply doing the housework.

Noticing his presence

> When Jacob awoke from his sleep, he thought, 'Surely the LORD is in this place, and I was not aware of it.' He was afraid and said, 'How awesome is this place! This is none other than the house of God; this is the gate of heaven' (Gen. 28:16,17).

I love the sense of awakening that Jacob experienced to God's presence and his immediate reaction of awe. Up to this point he knew of God but had no personal encounter with him, but God had a plan and was watching over his life to fulfil it, despite the fact that Jacob was a cheat and had stolen his brother's blessing.

Earlier it said that 'Jacob left Beersheba and set out for Harran. When he reached a certain place, he stopped for the night because the sun had set' (vv. 10,11).

What amazes me is the incidental nature of Jacob's decision to stop. It was a circumstantial decision based on the time of day and his need to rest. As far as Jacob was concerned, he was just being sensible. He stopped where he was in the midst of the desert, picked up a stone that was at hand, lay down and went to sleep. The account doesn't refer to him praying or seeking the Lord's wisdom as to where to stop or what to do. He was just living his life and deciding things on the go as so many of us do.

But this was described as 'a certain place', not just anywhere. The key is that humanly there was nothing about this place that made it stand out. It had no name, special buildings or sacred mountain. It was just a place. But because Jacob was there, God was there with him. And because he was there with him, that ordinary place became a sacred place. Any place can become a sacred place when we recognise that God is there with us. God wanted to show Jacob that he was loved and sought after by God. He came to him in a dream once Jacob was asleep and resting his mind and body. It was from that place of rest that God was able to communicate to Jacob with the result that he became personally aware of the presence of God for the first time.

A personal illustration

Some years ago, Marilyn and I had a friend to visit. When it was time for her to return home, we accompanied her to the station. We were early so decided to wait in a nearby park and pray together. We sat on the grass and while Elizabeth was praying, an amazing thought popped into my mind.

'Do you realise that this is sacred ground?'

I was shocked. This was just a rather tatty patch of grass on the edge of a recreation ground. How could it be sacred?

'Because you are praying together, I have come to be with you in a special way. Because of that, the very ground you are sitting on has become a sacred place.'

I looked around me. Marilyn and Elizabeth were still praying. A few metres away some children were playing alongside young couples pushing baby buggies. Dog walkers strolled along . . . How could this be a holy place? Was I imagining things? Then another thought came to me: 'Because of your prayers, I am touching all these passers-by with my love.'

Surely that couldn't be right? 'Lord, I wasn't even aware of people passing and certainly wasn't praying for them!' I protested.

'When you invited me to be in the midst of you by praying together, this whole area became holy because I am here with you. Because of that, my Spirit is able to bless all those passing by. They are walking through a sacred place and I am touching them with my love.'

I was stunned by this as it had never occurred to me that our general prayers could release the presence of God to those around us, especially when we hardly know they are there. This revelation has transformed my prayer life.

Where we are, God is

In Jacob's story there is a telling phrase that applies to us all.

Jacob states in his amazement: 'Surely the LORD is in this place, and I was not aware of it' (v. 16).

I feel really challenged as I think about those words. How often do we just get on with our lives unaware that he is with us and that therefore the very place we are in has become holy? We agree that God knows all about us, but what does that mean in reality? Is he spying on us? Is he like a portrait on the wall staring down at us, present in the room but with no life or connection? Is he asleep or disinterested? There is a story in Mark 4:35–40, where Jesus was literally asleep during a storm and the disciples panicked and felt he didn't care. They looked at the circumstances and felt paralysed by fear instead of challenged by the faith adventure they had suddenly found themselves in.

> ... A furious squall came up, and the waves broke over the boat, so that it was nearly swamped. Jesus was in the stern, sleeping on a cushion. The disciples woke him and said to him, 'Teacher, don't you care if we drown?'
>
> He got up, rebuked the wind and said to the waves, 'Quiet! Be still!' Then the wind died down and it was completely calm.
>
> He said to his disciples, 'Why are you so afraid? Do you still have no faith?'

Are you like the disciples, living in anxiety, weighed down by your circumstances and feeling overwhelmed? Does the fact that he is with you seem more like an abstract idea than a vital reality? Does he seem to be detached from your situation, asleep and uncaring?

But just as those disciples discovered, Jesus is always in control, and even when we can't discern his presence and his help seems far away, he is so much greater than anything we may be going through. He was able to sleep during the storm because he was totally secure in his Father's love. Some of his disciples were experienced fishermen and knew the Sea of Galilee well. They were tough working men but, even for the toughest of us, life can whip the ground from under our feet; the most important thing we can do then, is to focus on the love of our heavenly Father and his powerful presence with us. There will be times when even our areas of expertise are not sufficient to help us and we become helpless like little children. But in that moment he is there and calls us to relax, trust and even to sleep.

If he is with us, he is in control

When those tough situations hit us, the scariest part can be the feeling that we don't have the answers or ability to resolve what's going on. This was why the fishermen panicked in the storm. Humanly they were helpless, but all Jesus needed to do was speak to the storm and it calmed down. His words 'Quiet! Be still!' released God's power to work, and his power is always far greater than any storm. As much as his presence is a source of comfort, so it is also the source of incredibly creative power; the power of his kingdom coming on earth as it is in heaven.

In Exodus 3, when God meets with Moses in the desert and calls him to lead the enslaved Israelites out of Egypt, and again in Joshua 1 when God commissions Joshua to take the baton from Moses to lead Israel into the promised land, God's reassurance to both men is 'I will be with you' (Exod. 3:12), and 'Do not be afraid; do not be discouraged, for the LORD your God will be with you wherever you go' (Josh. 1:9).

Through Moses and Joshua choosing to trust in his promise to be with them, amazing power was released and the history of the Israelites changed forever. This promise was not just for these mighty men; it is for us too, for we are the ones who have been raised up to be his present-day ambassadors.

'I will be with you,' says God to you and me.

I know that I really want to take hold of this, my Father's promise and see his power released to change my own storms and even the world's history, just as they did.

Thankfulness and rejoicing

As we draw near to the end of this chapter, I want us to focus on a wonderful way for us to enter into the joy of him being with us; the way of thankfulness and rejoicing.

My heart leaps for joy, and with my song I praise him (Ps. 28:7).

Worshipping him, rejoicing in his goodness even in the midst of life's storms and thanking him for his loving answers are all keys to knowing him and his power at work in our lives. Paul exhorts us in Philippians 4:4–6:

> Rejoice in the LORD always. I will say it again: rejoice! Let your gentleness be evident to all. The LORD is near. Do not be anxious about anything.

Do you see that promise again? 'The LORD is near.' This is the reason we can rejoice. We are not being naïve optimists but joyful realists. It's interesting that Paul drops in the phrase about our gentleness. At a casual reading it doesn't seem to fit, but then I realised how short-tempered we can get when we feel overwhelmed by situations. But when we focus upon his presence with us, rejoicing in him and all that he is to us, our habitual responses change and become Christlike. The following is a personal story from everyday life, précised from my book *Flying Free with God*.

> I was waiting for a bus that showed no sign of coming. I was fed up and felt like giving someone a belting! When I eventually got home I had to empty the bin and spent several minutes trying to prise a black bin liner open. In my frustration I shook it so hard that it crackled loudly, terrifying the cat!
>
> Suddenly a thought dropped into my mind:
>
> 'What a grumpy old bag *you* are! Where's your thankfulness?'
>
> I was shocked, the bin liner hanging limply from my hand. It hadn't even occurred to me to be thankful that irritating day.
>
> 'There's no one around so why bother!' was my muttered reaction.
>
> Have you ever realised God speaks through silence?
>
> This was a real silence as if a loud CD was suddenly turned off; the silence of his presence. And I knew it was his hurt presence. I had just called him 'Nobody' and dismissed all reasons for thanking him. And there were many reasons – ways he'd already shown me his love that day.

'Lord, I am so sorry.'

I knew that he still loved me, but longed for me to have a wider vision. How could I have been so miserable about silly things like buses and bin bags when *he* was at my side all the time? There were so many beautiful things all around me that he longed to draw my attention to, if only I looked.

'Lord, please give me that wider vision. I am sorry for being a moaner. Help me to become your joy catcher and spreader.'

Later, I stood at the bus stop again and the bus was late. Tension was rising but I suddenly remembered my prayer. I silently welcomed him at my side and asked him to give me childlike eyes to see his joy. Suddenly my eye was drawn to a boy of about nine walking with his mum. He was holding her hand and skipping. I felt Jesus' great pleasure in his happy closeness to his mum and his freedom to enjoy childlike pleasures.

A very old lady, bent double, struggled to get off a bus, a line of people waiting behind her, one a teenage boy. He pushed towards the old lady and I tensed thinking he was going to shove her aside. But he offered her his arm and helped her down. I felt the Lord had tears in his eyes as he rejoiced in this youth's kindness. My own eyes filled as I realised how present the Lord is in all that is happening around us. He longs for us to see with his eyes of love and respond from his heart of joy.[2]

 **Pause and reflect**

- Thinking of these stories: Jesus in the boat with his disciples, Moses, Joshua and finally me in my bad mood, what was God trying to teach us all to understand?
- Would you say that you are daily aware of God's presence with you?
- If you are struggling right now, spend some time thanking him that he is with you. If need be, ask him for forgiveness for focusing more on the problem than on him and his promise to help you.

- Ask him to help you to see life from his perspective and so become a joy spreader to those around you.
- Spend some time rejoicing in these prophetic words from Marilyn's song 'Rest in My Love':

Rest in my love, relax in my care
And know that my presence will always be there.
You are my child and I care for you
There's nothing my love and my power cannot do.

Marilyn Baker

Extract taken from the song 'Rest in My Love' by Marilyn Baker (Authentic). Copyright © 1982 Authentic Publishing.*

7

Getting to Know Your Father

Philip said, 'Lord, show us the Father and that will be enough for us.' Jesus answered: 'Don't you know me, Philip, even after I have been among you such a long time? Anyone who has seen me has seen the Father.'

John 14:8,9

Is there a gulf in your understanding?

Are you like Philip, struggling to join the dots in what you know in your head and what you experience in your heart? Do you wonder if faith is just a mental theory that will only transform into reality when we meet him face-to-face? The ironic thing is that when Philip blurted out those haunting words, he inadvertently highlighted the primary purpose of Jesus coming, to restore us back into relationship with the Father.

Philip couldn't put it into words, but he knew there was a gulf in his understanding. He knew Scripture, he had faith. He worshipped God and had lived as one of Jesus' closest friends for three years. He had seen the miracles, heard the teaching, felt the compassion, seen demonic powers destroyed and prisons of sickness done away with. He'd watched Jesus embracing dirty children, affirming prostitutes and giving dead bodies new life.

Every day had shattered his perceptions, yet . . . there was still a gulf in his understanding. He wanted to know the Father. He wanted to see, experience and connect with God like Jesus did. But somehow, he hadn't made the emotional and mental connection that through Jesus, his longing was already being fulfilled. As Jesus said in John 14:6,7:

I am the way and the truth and the life. No one comes to the Father except through me. If you really know me, you would know my Father as well.

Jesus points us to the Father and reveals perfectly what he is like. He expected his friends to recognise the Father in all he said and did. He listened to his Father's voice and then spoke the Father's words, bringing compassion and love to all. It's vital we realise that we too can daily grow into a deeper experience of the Father as we take time to look at the Son. But many of us struggle like Philip to reconcile what we know with what we experience. The key is the Holy Spirit. Despite being privy to Jesus' teaching and miracles, all the disciples were confused until the Holy Spirit was poured out at Pentecost. He then gave them understanding and transformed their head knowledge to heart experience. He promises us this same transformation. Listen to Jesus' words in John 14:16–18:

> And I will ask the Father, and he will give you another advocate to help you and be with you for ever – the Spirit of truth. The world cannot accept him, because it neither sees him nor knows him. But you know him, for he lives with you and will be in you. I will not leave you as orphans; I will come to you.

'I will not leave you as orphans.' Our orphan spirit cries out because we were created for a love relationship with God and nothing else can fill that gap; not even the best things in life, such as marrying or having children. We are all crying out to know what our Father is like. The key is to understand that Jesus perfectly reveals who the Father is, and it's the Holy Spirit's work to make Jesus known to us.

Personal story

When I was first a Christian I felt a constant heartache through believing I was a failure and unlovable. I would often cry silently all night, I just felt so empty. Friends would say, 'God loves you, Tracy.' But I couldn't feel that love. As I've already shared, I had very few memories of my dad, although I could remember watching one day as he returned from shopping, carrying a basket from which I could see a little puppy's golden head poking out. I loved Penny the corgi and she became a huge comfort in later years when my life got very tough. Knowing it was my dad who bought her for my sister and I to enjoy having a pet was also a precious thing.

After my dad died, the hurts I then experienced through my stepfather, plus the isolation of deafness, exacerbated my inner pain and in a sense gave a name to it too, so that if I went for prayer ministry it was those issues that were focused upon. Rightly so, for they had left deep wounds and there was no way I could relax into being God's beloved daughter until they were healed.

However, I had a need beyond those hurts, this same need that Philip expresses to Jesus, 'Lord, show us the Father.' I did need healing of abuse and shame, but for transformation to really last, I needed to know my heavenly Father's love from my heart.

Blind eyes and shuttered hearts

Even today I am still aware of a kind of walled-off area in my emotions and memories as if I don't know quite how to experience life and love. Maybe you too find it impossible to imagine emotionally connecting with God as Father? We can withdraw from him, like the elder brother in the prodigal son story when he talked about slaving for his father all his life. This son hadn't recognised his father's loving and giving nature because he was blinded by his own negativity and self-righteousness. Coldness, inability to love, drivenness, judgementalism, resentment, envy and bitterness were all symptoms of his disconnection. We too can display such symptoms when our feelings are locked away because of hurts or the sins that we've failed to bring to the Lord for forgiveness.

But God *can* release us from that prison. Zacchaeus, in Luke 19:1–10 is a wonderful example of someone starting to heed his heart hunger to see Jesus but still feeling the need to hide. He wants to see but not to be seen. But coming into true intimacy with God always begins with realising we are seen and known from the inside out and yet still loved. Jesus stops under Zacchaeus's hiding place and calls his name, not judgementally but in compassion and love:

> When Jesus reached the spot, he looked up and said to him, 'Zacchaeus, come down immediately. I must stay at your house today.' So he came down at once and welcomed him gladly.

 Pause and reflect

Do you identify with Zacchaeus? His sense of shame, despite his wealth, was obviously acute. Not many of us will literally hide away in a tree, but we do hide behind façades that seem more acceptable. So the older brother hid behind his slavish hard work, the Pharisees and Sadducees hid behind their religiosity, the Samaritan woman hid from her community by collecting water when no one else would be about, Martha hid behind her respectability and busyness . . . These examples bring home that the Father always calls us into the light, even with the things that cause us deep shame, because he desires to free us from their devastating effect. When people grumbled about Zacchaeus, Jesus silenced them with these amazing words:

> Today salvation has come to this house, because this man, too, is a son of Abraham (Luke 19:9).

This was the Father's kiss of love to a man hiding away in his sinfulness and hurt. Firstly, Jesus called Zacchaeus by name, communicating that he was fully known. Secondly, he wanted to stay with Zacchaeus, communicating real friendship. Thirdly, he gave him a new identity: 'son of Abraham', communicating that Zacchaeus was as much a beloved son as the rest of them.

Jesus' love had a powerful effect. Zacchaeus came out of denial about his past sinful choices and instantly wanted to make restitution.

> Look, Lord! Here and now I give half of my possessions to the poor, and if I have cheated anybody out of anything, I will pay back four times the amount (Luke 19:8).

The Lord will give you a new name

Jesus gave Zacchaeus a new name. This love ministry was prophesied in Isaiah 62:2–5:

> The Lord will give you a new name. The Lord will hold you in his hands for all to see – a splendid crown in the hands of God. Never again will you be called Godforsaken or Desolate. Your new name will be: God's Delight and The Bride of God, for the Lord delights in you and will claim you as his own . . . Then God will rejoice over you as a bridegroom rejoices over his bride (précis of the NLT).

This promise is addressed to Zion, God's beloved holy city, but if we therefore distance ourselves from it, we are mistaken. In the Bible, God's promises, as indeed his judgements, always operated on several levels. So this passage was also looking forward prophetically to the new kingdom of believers in Jesus – in other words, to us.

Listen to these words from 1 Peter 2:9–10:

> But you are a chosen people, a royal priesthood, a holy nation, God's special possession, that you may declare the praises of him who called you out of darkness into his wonderful light. Once you were not a people, but now you are the people of God; once you had not received mercy, but now you have received mercy.

Peter is writing not just to Jews, but also to new believers in Jesus, whom he refers to as 'a holy nation'. While their old names may have been: Not Belonging, Unforgiven and Not a People, now God is renaming them: 'Chosen'; 'Royal'; 'Holy' . . .

The point is that our name in this context is synonymous with our identity. It is God's work of love through Jesus to break forever the power of that old, wounded identity and free us to live in the new.

What's in a name?

When I was about 13, I was walking home from school one day with my best friend and we got talking about our names. My friend had three Christian names with strong meanings like 'leader' and 'pearl'. This obviously made her very proud.

Rather wistfully I said, 'I don't think Tracy has any meaning, it's just a made-up name.'

She replied, 'It seems right that you've got a meaningless name.'

She went home but I stood staring after her. What had she meant? It had sounded so definite. Surely she didn't think I was such a meaningless person that I only merited a meaningless name? She was my best friend, after all. She must have just meant that I didn't need to be shackled down with a heavy traditional name.

I pushed aside the hurt feelings and forgot the conversation, or rather, it disappeared from my mind, but unknown to me it was still lurking in my subconscious. Not in the sense of an indignant 'What right did she have to say that?' but in that I believed I *was* meaningless. Her comment added to my ingrained self-rejection and I felt shame that she saw what I really was, a meaningless person.

Of course, none of this was really to do with a 13-year-old's tactless remark. Many other things were happening in my life which all conspired together to rob me of self-worth. As I grew into adulthood, it was as if I could feel something shrivelling inside me. My personhood, all that made me, *me* was gradually curling up, hiding her face and giving up on life.

Hating my name

It's amazing how deeply little things can affect us, for years later, even though now a Christian and in ministry, part of me still felt I was meaningless. Every time I introduced myself I felt silly. My name was frequently paired with Marilyn's when organisers announced us both at the start of a concert. The name 'Marilyn Baker' had a real ring to it while 'Tracy' just sounded trite. Why? What's in a name, after all? Why did it feel so pathetic and ineffectual when God loved me? But deep down I couldn't love myself, because that 'self' was Tracy.

I always felt that whenever I told someone my name, I was in effect confessing to being a washout. This was because despite all the healing and change God had brought me, I still believed negative things about myself. I often joked about my 'silly' name with others and started mock competitions to see who could think of the best new name. Temperance, Chastity and Innocence were all suggested!

But unknown to me, this aversion was a symptom of a much deeper truth. That while I had let God heal so many hurts and had thus taken many steps which I would never have thought possible, a deep part of me, the 'Tracy part' was still curled up in hiding, unable to believe that she was truly loved.

But wasn't all this just my problem?

You may be wondering why I am going into so much detail. Wasn't I just a depressive personality? Surely this kind of inward struggle isn't relevant to most people who would view themselves in a much more positive light?

Sadly, I don't think that is the case. Many people say they don't like their names, but more importantly it doesn't take long to discover just how much people dislike themselves. Often this is disguised by a bright smile, a serving heart, or an extrovert personality. Yet a secret inner part is curled up and locked away from life. It is that part that God longs to set free and heal.

◤ Pause and reflect

A little fun exercise – you will need to use your imagination for this and you may like to jot your answers/reflections in your journal.

- A long-awaited opportunity has arisen for you to meet a much-admired famous person (imagine who this might be – a film star? a Christian speaker? a singer? Jesus?).

- What emotions are you aware of as your turn to meet draws near?
- Now imagine them smiling at you and shaking hands. When they ask your name, how do you feel?
- What is your overriding reaction in answering their questions about yourself: Pleasure? Embarrassment? Awkwardness?
- Take some time to reflect over your responses. If your overriding feelings were happy, spend a few moments thanking the Lord that he has enabled you to be relaxed in your own identity. Ask him for the grace to see more clearly the unique gifts and personality traits that enable you to reflect him.
- If, on the other hand, your overriding feelings were nervousness or shame, talk to him about it. Don't try to analyse the feelings, just tell him you want to see yourself truly as he sees you.
- If you have written this in your journal, date the prayer so that in time you can look back and see how the Lord has changed you.

Hearing my true name

In a memorable church service a few years ago, my pastor shared about our special name from God, quoting the promise from Revelation 2:17:

> I will also give that person a white stone with a new name written on it, known only to the one who receives it.

This is not just a fancy idea, for God's special name for us both affirms the truth of who we are in him and empowers us to live as he created us to be.

My pastor sensed that God wanted to tell us our special names as we opened our hearts to listen. So along with all the others I went forward and waited quietly for God to speak to me. But instantly my mind was barraged with the negative names that I'd heard so often: Lazy, Unlovable, Stupid, Rubbish . . . The words burst into my consciousness like a hammer shattering a window and I felt overwhelmed by the helplessness that I'd constantly experienced as a child. I was a fool to think there could be any other name for me. I prayed in desperation: 'Lord, you know all these negative words. They feel true, but they're crushing me. I don't know what is you and what isn't any more. Please let me hear you. If you have a name for me that is different, please let me hear it.'

Quietness came over me. The negative words seemed distanced as if there was a protective moat around me. Suddenly I became aware of a beautiful phrase whispering in my mind, 'Daughter of Mercy.'

I was stunned. Could this really be God? Surely such a beautiful name couldn't be for me? Yet I knew that God could only speak words of truth and grace, never to crush and condemn. Even when I went wrong in life his rebuke would be in kindness and love. His word may pierce like a sharp sword but would never destroy me. God knew the truth about me, all he had made me to be and all he had dealt with on the cross for my sake. Couldn't I receive this as truly being from him?

Choosing to believe

In that situation I needed to choose to accept by faith that the name Daughter of Mercy was for me. The words had slipped so simply into my consciousness it was easy to dismiss them, yet I would never have thought of them myself. It was my Father affirming me as his precious daughter.

My pastor encouraged us to prayerfully reflect on anything that came to our minds and ask God to reveal its meaning. I was suddenly filled with joy. God my Father was saying that I truly did belong in his family and that he was proud to call me daughter. It's hard to describe the effect of this. I had so often felt an embarrassment to those around me. Now the word 'Daughter' was reaching that wound and bringing it out into the light. It was joy mixed with pain because these were feelings I had buried all my life. Yet I knew this was the way of healing and transformation.

The second part of the name, 'of Mercy' was also very meaningful. I knew it described the way that Jesus wanted me to reach out. He had shown me mercy in such incredible ways. He sought me out and worked in my life to bring healing, and in the process enabled me to start touching the lives of others through my ministry with Marilyn. Now he was confirming all that had happened and saying that I was to be someone who gave his mercy away to others, helping them to be changed and healed.[1]

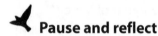 **Pause and reflect**

Read these words of Marilyn's song 'He Called My Name' and let Jesus minister his transforming love into your own hurts.

> He called my name and made me his own
> To him I am precious, a jewel in his crown.
> His blood has cleansed me, by him I'm loved and known
> And he says that I'll be with him on his throne.
>
> Marilyn Baker
>
> Extract taken from the song 'He Called My Name' by Marilyn Baker (Authentic). Copyright © 1985 Authentic Publishing.*

- Spend a few moments praying. Is there a hiding place in your own life that you'd like him to release you from?
- Read the song again and make the words your own. Ask him what your own special name is and listen quietly. He may whisper it into your heart. Thank him and receive it.

Rooted and established

Paul prays a wonderful, Spirit inspired prayer in Ephesians 3:14–19:

> For this reason I kneel before the Father, from whom every family in heaven and on earth derives its name. I pray that out of his glorious riches he may strengthen you with power through his Spirit in your inner being, so that Christ may dwell in your hearts through faith. And I pray that you,

being rooted and established in love, may have power, together with all the Lord's holy people, to grasp how wide and long and high and deep is the love of Christ, and to know this love that surpasses knowledge – that you may be filled to the measure of all the fullness of God.

What is Paul praying for us?

- That we know we belong and that God wants to strengthen and establish us in his love.
- In God's family everyone is named after him and everyone belongs.
- He is rich and out of his riches will strengthen us in our faith.
- He will root and establish us. These are nurturing words. Anyone who enjoys gardening will know the care that is needed to establish a new plant. They have to be nurtured. So he nurtures us, creating an inner power to experience his love with the whole of our lives.

A prophetic word

I've prayed so often for God to show me his Father heart. I can sense him saying that he loves to answer *all* our prayers, but the prayer to know him and his love brings him great joy to answer: He says prophetically to us all: 'I am your Father. I love you unconditionally. I can never stop loving you. I delight in you. You are beautiful to me. I love to be with you. I feel your pain and love to comfort you. I gave my Son that you would be free of all that has crippled you and that you would belong to me forever. I love to lavish my love on you, to quiet you with my lullaby of love, to affirm, excite and challenge you. Let me be your daddy.'

Spend a few moments drinking in the truth of his love for you.

Steps to recognising the Father's love

Are we excited about discovering what the Father is like? Jesus would get up early and go off to be alone with his Father. He would meditate on what the Scriptures revealed about him and would listen for his voice and seek deeper revelation. His everyday life was a window giving glimpses into God's character; for instance, when he saw children asking their parents for food, he allowed this familiar scene to open his heart to the Father's desire to answer our prayers. When shepherds searched for their lost sheep, he understood his Father's passion to seek out those who are lost and rescue them. In Matthew 6, he tells his followers not to worry about their lives because if their Father has made tiny flowers with such extravagant attention to detail and provided for birds, making them carefree and full of joy, how much more will he provide for his children because of their far greater value to him?

Jesus calls us to listen in the same way

Are our own hearts open to this kind of revelation? The beauty of creation, our jobs and ordinary situations of family life are all possible channels for him to speak through. In that example of the flowers and birds, Jesus said 'look' at them. His friends needed to stop what they were doing, look at what was around them and take time to think, noticing, for example, that the flowers were extravagantly coloured – then asking God to speak to them.

This is a key for us to live life in an adventurous way knowing that anything can become a channel for us to hear his voice.

 Pause and reflect

- Take some time to be with the Lord and have a pen and paper to hand.
- Tell him you want to hear his voice and grow deeper in your understanding of him.
- If it's a nice day, have a wander outside or look at what's around you, what catches your eye – it could be anything: a leaf, a cloud, a pile of washing up, a picture . . .

- Take time to look at it in its context like Jesus did with the flowers and birds. Use your senses – listen, touch, look.
- Ask your Father, 'Lord, what do you want me to understand about you through what I'm seeing or experiencing now?' Write down anything that comes to you.
- Then ask him, 'Lord what do you want to say to me through this?' Remember, he speaks to build you up and his words will be loving even if challenging, so ignore any negative thoughts. Treasure any insights that come and write them down.

8

Revelation of the Father's Love

The Spirit you received does not make you slaves, so that you live in fear again; rather, the Spirit you received brought about your adoption to sonship. And by him we cry, 'Abba, Father.'

Rom. 8:15

The spirit of sonship

We have received the Spirit of sonship, the Holy Spirit our counsellor who gives us revelation and understanding of God. This is mind-boggling because what we cannot do for ourselves, God does for us by sending his Spirit into our hearts, empowering us to shout aloud with joy when we understand we have become God's beloved children:

And by him we cry, '*Abba*, Father.'

Jesus called his Father '*Abba*,' the Hebrew for Daddy or Papa. Even today, Jewish children run to their fathers calling out, '*Abba, Abba*.' It's a cry of belonging, of trust and delight in their father's company. Paul goes on to say:

The Spirit himself testifies with our spirit that we are God's children (8:16).

Think of that word 'testify'. It's to do with speaking the truth. You may be asked to testify about someone's character in court. You need to give a true character reference or description of what that person did on a certain day. Or you may be asked to testify against someone, to tell the truth about what they have done to hurt you or someone else. Recently, a sportsman went public to tell of being abused as a child by his coach. His testimony opened the floodgates and sportsmen everywhere started testifying to similar experiences. This experience of testifying to the truth was cathartic, allowing them to start on the road to healing.

In a similar way, when Paul describes the Spirit as 'testifying with our spirit' he is describing a process of communication between the Holy Spirit and our own spirits. The Spirit's work is to speak God's truth into our hearts that we belong to God and are unconditionally loved. He is constantly at work to make the love of God known to us. Listen to what Jesus said about the Holy Spirit in John 14:25–27 and 16:13,14. You may like to read and reflect upon the whole of chapters 14 – 17 as there is so much more that Jesus teaches us about the Holy Spirit.

> All this I have spoken while still with you. But the Advocate, the Holy Spirit, whom the Father will send in my name, will teach you all things and will remind you of everything I have said to you. Peace I leave with you; my peace I give you.

> But when he, the Spirit of truth, comes, he will guide you into all the truth. He will not speak on his own; he will speak only what he hears, and he will tell you what is yet to come. He will glorify me because it is from me that he will receive what he will make known to you.

I feel joy bubbling up inside me. What an amazing gift from God who does not call us to live our Christian lives in a rule-directed way, but as friends through the Holy Spirit communicating with us. He makes God's Word alive to us and guides and empowers us and gives us revelation of areas of our lives that need healing.

Divine comfort through Spirit revelation

The following story was contributed by a friend, Teresa, who experienced Father's compassionate love during a time of struggle in her life.

I have suffered with ME and Fibromyalgia since getting Meningitis in 2005. The everyday pain I experience occasionally gets the better of me and as I tire so easily I feel my life has no purpose. Sometimes I wonder how anyone can see me as anything but a waste of space.

When spending time with Jesus, I like to imagine myself in a garden with him. I went there recently, when I was feeling particularly useless, and as I entered the garden, in the spirit so to speak, I saw Jesus sitting on a bench waiting for me. I went up to him and sat down and he asked me what was troubling me. I told him about how useless I felt and he simply looked deeply into my eyes and said, 'Would you care to dance?'

I said I would love to but I couldn't. He drew me into his arms and whispered, 'Dance with me. I'll lead; all you have to do is relax and follow me.' We began to dance and as I relaxed and followed where he led me, the weight I was carrying just seemed to melt away. He kept eye contact as if to reassure me that he wouldn't let me go and he whispered, 'I love dancing with you. To me you are precious, my bride, and all I want you to do is let me lead and you follow.' As we finished, he leaned in and kissed me on my forehead, put his hand on my cheek and smiled. I knew I was loved and felt like I could take on the world.

Pause and reflect

- How did that story make you feel? Does it resonate with anything going on in your own life?
- Following talking with Jesus and then dancing with him, Teresa knew she was loved. It is a beautiful encounter, a picture of his tenderness and ability to lift us up and give us a new focus. God has no favourites. Can you imagine him meeting with you in a similarly tender way?
- Try imaginatively sitting in a garden with him as Teresa did, telling him what's on your heart and letting him respond.
- What did he say?
- What did he do?

- How did you respond?
- Write in your journal what happened.

Peace

As Jesus spoke about the Holy Spirit he said 'my peace I give you'. Knowing God loves us brings us deep peace and frees us from fear. So Paul taught us in Romans 8 that 'The Spirit you received does not make you slaves, so that you live in fear again'. Our Father knows the issues we contend with and the fears we face, but he is promising that through the ministry of the Holy Spirit we can know a true inner peace and the joy of relationship. The key is believing God has given us all we need to know him in an ever-deepening way.

A transforming vision

A friend called Lilian had a very tough upbringing and as a result found it impossible to connect with God as Father. As an adult she experienced times of deep depression and although she had been a Christian since childhood, there was a vast gulf between what she knew about God and what she experienced from her heart. She felt despairing as any talk of God's Fatherhood seemed completely unreal to her. Lilian started attending our conferences and one day to her utter amazement, the Holy Spirit gave her a vision of Father God and the heavenly realm that totally transformed her understanding. Here is her testimony in her own words:

> I grew up feeling like my parents' possession and not a person. Consequently, as an adult I didn't know how to be a person and never knew how to conceive of God as Father. My father was always very authoritarian when at home where he ruled with an iron fist or a leather belt and had no time for any of us.

I'd had a lot of teaching about God as Father but I just couldn't picture that Person other Christians talked about. He was almighty, that wasn't a problem. Creator, in control, my father had been all these things, but not caring or loving in any way. Then on the 6th August I met Father God. I was astonished to find him the most joyful . . . well, his eyes shone with merriment. His face was one big smile and warmth and love oozed from him. And he was so proud of his children and what we were doing for him. My earthly father never showed any interest, never even acknowledged any good thing I did, but Father God was proclaiming me his to all of heaven. He looked upon us all, saying to the angels, 'Look at them; aren't they great?' He said it again, 'Aren't they great?' He then encouraged me to go on doing what he had for me to do.

The next morning as a group of us prayed together, I watched as he listened intently to our prayers and sent his angels scurrying to answer. He was showing me a glimpse into heaven, to see just how much he cared about his children because his Son came from glory to die on a cross to make us his sons and daughters.

I know now that he loves us, all of us.[1]

The Holy Spirit was transforming Lilian's perception of God

Through these visions, the Holy Spirit gently overcame the pain of Lilian's childhood, transporting her into a new reality where she was able to experience her heavenly Father. It is awesome how she saw the merriment on his face and heard the pride in his voice. Such attributes were so alien to her that only God could have given her such revelation. I find it beautiful, and having known her for many years can testify to its powerful effect; for she truly is someone who knows the Father's heart, and since then has had many amazing visions and words, bringing healing to other hurting people.

Pause and reflect

- How does this vision of Father God's joy and pride in us make you feel?
- If this description of him is counter to your past experiences, pray that he will open your eyes to see him as he truly is, full of loving kindness and joy.

Vision into the heavenlies

What Lilian experienced in that transforming encounter is the realm of truth that we cannot see with our natural eyes but can see with the eyes of faith, through the Holy Spirit giving us revelation. This is for us all, as Joel prophesied:

> And afterwards, I will pour out my Spirit on all people. Your sons and daughters will prophesy, your old men will dream dreams, your young men will see visions. Even on my servants, both men and women, I will pour out my Spirit in those days (Joel 2:28,29).

God is saying that not one of us is exempt from receiving the gift of his Spirit. The Spirit's language is characterised by love and peace and is in the form of insight, knowledge, visions, dreams and prophecy. He himself is our teacher and will open our eyes to his Word. In 2 Kings 6:15–17 we see how an ordinary man's eyes were opened to see the power of God's army:

> When the servant of the man of God got up and went out early the next morning, an army with horses and chariots had surrounded the city. 'Oh no, my lord! What shall we do?' the servant asked.
>
> 'Don't be afraid,' the prophet answered. 'Those who are with us are more than those who are with them.'
>
> And Elisha prayed, 'Open his eyes, LORD, so that he may see.' Then the LORD opened the servant's eyes, and he looked and saw the hills full of horses and chariots of fire all round Elisha.

A simple prayer of faith opened the servant's eyes to the heavenly realm. Keep praying that the Holy Spirit will open your eyes in the same way.

How does the Holy Spirit make the Father known to us?

Jesus described the Holy Spirit as counselling us, guiding us, speaking to us, making God known, convicting us and reminding us of Jesus' words.

I experienced this in an amazing way when God spoke to me as I was walking to college soon after becoming a Christian. I lived near a beautiful golf course and walked past its lovely views every day, but never noticed because of my anxieties. Being endlessly belittled as I grew up created a framework for how I saw myself, and out of that I responded fearfully, expecting others to reject me. This then impacted on how I related to them. Every time someone spoke sharply, I took it as confirmation that I was rubbish. Even after becoming a Christian I still felt shame at root level. As Paul describes, I was a slave to fear. I knew God loved me and I had accepted Jesus' forgiveness, but needed something big to happen at the core to change me. What happened next was a glimpse into God's desire to set us free from past hurts and wrong mindsets.

Jesus constantly listened for the Holy Spirit's revelation. We need that too and on this particular day as I walked to college, I felt a sudden urge to stop and look around me.

Rather grumpily I gazed across the fields. The sun was shining and little clouds were scudding across the sky. There was a warm breeze, the expectation of spring. Suddenly I noticed that everything seemed newer and brighter; the grass greenly glittering, the tiny wildflowers full of colour, the trees majestic. As I gazed I sensed God there with me and I realised it was him who had nudged me to stop. Then a clear thought came to me with such clarity that I knew it had to be him speaking: 'I made all this so you could know what I am like, but none of this is as beautiful to me as you are.'

I was stunned and the wall around my heart began to crumble away. It was just a tiny chink but this was one of my first steps into inner transformation. God was breaking the power of fear and shame by telling me I was beautiful to him.

The Spirit revealed the Father's character

This experience helped me understand that God speaks through creation and shows us what he is like. The more we see the beauty of all he has made, the more we will discover his goodness and love.

Interestingly, I then began to talk with God about my stepfather, feeling I needed to let go of the tremendous hurts he had caused me. I wanted to see my stepfather through God's eyes. After praying like this for a few weeks, I was visiting home one day and noticed how beautiful the garden looked. The thought came that it was in this way that my stepfather most showed that he was made in God's image. My first reaction was revulsion as, despite my prayers, I still felt he was a monster and surely couldn't be made in God's image? I angrily shut my eyes to the beauty and what God seemed be saying through it. But the thought persisted and I found myself thinking of Genesis 1:26,27:

> Then God said, 'Let us make man in our image, in our likeness . . . ' So God created mankind in his own image, in the image of God he created him; male and female he created them.

Humankind had been made in God's image. In other words, there was something about God in everyone. This was a truth I didn't want to hear. I felt I had a right to judge my stepfather and I just couldn't see any good in him. But after stewing angrily for a while I prayed again, and sensed God gently showing me that it was impossible for him to make anything bad. All creation was good and humankind was the pinnacle. Of course, the fall means that we all constantly make wrong choices and need Jesus to forgive and bring alive God's loveliness in us, but his likeness is within us all.

As the Holy Spirit showed me this, I started to pray: 'Father, you know I have hated him. I am sorry. Thank you that you made him in your image. Thank you that he makes beautiful gardens. Please help me to see him as you see him and to forgive him like you've forgiven me.'

Father God was transforming me, helping me to understand his tender love for all and to let him change my hard heart.

 Pause and reflect

- Is there anyone in your life whose actions have wounded you?
- How do you feel towards them? (Be real, God already knows.)
- Spend a few minutes quietly acknowledging those feelings as if you're holding them before you on open palms.
- If you can, tell your Father you don't want to carry them any more and ask him to help you let them go.
- Listen for his voice: he may draw you to a scripture that gives you a new perspective, or give you a sense of deep peace. He may affirm you like when he spoke to me through the landscape. He may nudge you to forgive the person or do something for them . . .
- Thank him for his loving work in your life.

The importance of his affirmation

Every child hungers for their dad's approval. It enables them to grow into mature adults, so when God told me I was beautiful to him, it filled a need that my earthly dad and stepfather could never meet. It was a fulfilment of the promise of God's blessings expressed by David in Psalm 103:1–5:

> . . . who forgives all your sins and heals all your diseases, who redeems your life from the pit and crowns you with love and compassion, who satisfies your desires with good things so that your youth is renewed like the eagle's.

David was encouraging his innermost being to know that God is good and compassionate, forgiving, restoring and answering our prayers in such a way that our youthfulness is renewed. David knew rejection – his own dad, Jesse, didn't even include him in the line-up of his sons when Samuel came to anoint one of them as king. That kind of rejection causes us to wall off our hearts and locks us into negative mindsets. We know from different Bible accounts that David felt the pain of his father's treatment; for example, in Psalm 27:9–10:

> Do not reject or forsake me, God my Saviour. Though my father and mother forsake me, the LORD will receive me.

David had an inner wound which was causing fear, not just about his parents but about whether God was *really* there for him. Sometimes God can seem very unreal, but David made a choice to walk in partnership with the truth of God's faithfulness rather than the negative whisper from his hurts. By the psalm's end he was joyfully declaring:

> I remain confident of this: I will see the goodness of the LORD in the land of the living.

Fake news

Since the inauguration of Donald Trump as US president there have been a lot of allegations about key people and nations such as Russia having a hold over him. In response Trump has declared several times that this was fake news. Those words resounded with me. It's a good phrase that we can use to stand against all the lies the enemy constantly bombards us with. In Trump's situation there were certain things that made it quite plausible that the allegations were true. It is the same when the enemy attacks us with his lies and innuendos. They can seem plausible, almost like absolute facts. So if our dad was not there for us, it is easy to believe the lie that God won't be there for us either. If Mum or Dad were dismissive of work we proudly brought home from school, it seems a fact that God won't be interested in what we do either.

I remember Krystal, a beautiful young woman who was repeatedly told by her mum that she was ugly and would never marry. Despite knowing the Lord, having lots of friends and achieving in her career, Krystal was constantly full of anxiety about how she looked and what people thought of her. In prayer ministry she always referred to her mum's words as if they were the absolute truth and responded with a *but* to every suggestion that the Lord loved her and saw her as beautiful. Sadly she never made the choice to dismiss her mum's words as 'fake news' and tragically died of cancer about three years after we met her, still believing she was ugly.

Meeting Father through his words

God's love is so vast and his words so powerful there is no doubt he can transform the deepest pain in our lives, but he cannot force such healing upon us. If all we've known is negatives, he knows we can't instantly start thinking positively, but we do at least need to tell him that we *want* to choose his truth over the lies of the enemy. Our Father will work with that desire and will feed us with the truth and start to bring us into a new place.

Listen to these verses about the power of God's words:

How sweet are your words to my taste, sweeter than honey to my mouth! (Ps. 119:103).

Your word is a lamp to my feet, a light on my path (Ps. 119:105).

As for God, his way is perfect: the LORD's word is flawless; he shields all who take refuge in him (Ps. 18:30).

For the word of God is alive and active. Sharper than any double-edged sword, it penetrates even to dividing soul and spirit, joints and marrow; it judges the thoughts and attitudes of the heart (Heb. 4:12).

An amusing anecdote

I remember years ago when I was volunteering at a holiday for the elderly during college summer break, I was going out with a fellow student called Tim at the time but hadn't heard from him as this was before texting and I cannot hear on the phone. One day, just as we were taking the guests for a walk, one of the staff gave me an envelope. It was from Tim and I was so excited. I was in charge of a wheelchair so, holding it with one hand, I ripped the envelope open and drew the letter out. I knew I'd read it properly later but just wanted to see a few phrases. I hardly noticed that the road was sloping downwards as I spread the letter out. The first words I saw were 'I love you' and 'I'm missing you'! I shrieked and couldn't wait to tell someone. Still not noticing the slope, I began to hurry to catch the others up and the chair started racing along at a great pace. We reached the others, but I couldn't slow the chair down and the footrests rammed into the ankles of the volunteer ahead of me. She was soon hopping around and neither she nor my disabled lady were very happy with me, but all I could think about were those words: 'I love you and I'm missing you.' Although it wasn't very sensible to race down a slope while in charge of a wheelchair, the fact remains that being told that I was loved released something within me, a joy of living and freedom from inhibition that wasn't, at that time, my natural way of being.

If a love letter from a boyfriend could have such an effect, how much more powerful are God's words to us? We can sometimes feel bored with the Bible and reluctant to spend time reading it, but Father God wants to meet us in its words. Remember, Hebrews 4:12 describes the Bible as being 'alive and active'. God's presence is in the words he inspired. We can read it superficially like we might read the newspaper, or we can come to it with an expectation that God is going to highlight a word, phrase or chapter, and as we talk and listen to him, he will show us something amazing.

God's Word is so rich

God's Word is rich in its power, authority and goodness. We saw how Psalm 119 describes it as sweeter than honey. Many of us love sweet things and find that honey (or chocolate) creates a real sense of contentment and satisfaction. The sweetness is comforting and makes us want to sample more. So, through this verse, God is telling us that his Word will bring us joy, satisfaction, contentment and yet also hunger: a good hunger for him and his love, a hunger that will call us to keep searching for him. Listen to these verses from Proverbs 2:1–5 about the attitude of anticipation he wants us to have as we search for him.

> My son, if you accept my words and store up my commands within you, turning your ear to wisdom and applying your heart to understanding – indeed, if you call out for insight and cry aloud for understanding, and if you look for it as for silver and search for it as for hidden treasure, then you will understand the fear of the LORD and find the knowledge of God.

 Pause and reflect

- What do the words 'silver' and 'hidden treasure' mean to you?
- Treasure can come in all shapes and forms, not just money and jewels. For example, a treasure may be art, possessions, experiences, freedom, success, family, healing, friendship . . . anything that we live for.
- What is your treasure and what would you give for it?
- It's important for us to acknowledge our desires as our Father loves to 'satisfy our desires with good things' (see Ps. 103:5).
- If you hold up that longing for your particular treasure and then re-read the above passage from Proverbs, what do you think the Lord is saying to you through it?

Searching

A key word in that Proverbs passage was 'search'. What does the concept of 'searching' suggest to you? Marilyn often loses things and I can feel 'Oh dear' when she calls out: 'Trace, I can't find my iPhone . . . '

As I have described earlier, I put my glasses down all the time and forget where. Searching for things when you think you won't find them can infuse the experience with anxiety. Once I was opening Christmas presents and my mum had sent me a cheque together with some chocolates. Later, I couldn't find the cheque. I was in a panic and tore my bedroom and office apart trying to find it. I turned the recycle crate out and went through every scrap of paper, but no cheque. Marilyn and our guests were all helping but I was dreading having to tell my mum that I'd lost her gift as soon as I'd opened it. Suddenly I sensed the Lord whispering to me to relax, that the cheque was in a safe place and to enjoy Christmas day with our guests. It took a few minutes to obey that loving directive, but I gradually stopped rushing round and relaxed into the loving atmosphere. There were still some presents under the tree, and suddenly I found my gaze drawn to one in particular. I knew it couldn't be anything to do with the cheque as I'd already had that, but I casually went to have a look. As soon as it was in my hand I realised it was my mum's gift of chocolates. The wrapping paper was only partially opened and when I pulled it aside I was amazed to discover the envelope with the missing cheque still in it. It was only then I remembered that when I'd been opening it, a visitor had arrived so I'd put the half-opened present back under the tree. The Lord was right, the gift was safe and I needn't have panicked for I found what I was searching for.

Jesus exhorted us to 'seek and you will find' (Matt. 7:7). He is calling us to search with the expectation that we will find what we are looking for, the growing experience of his love and friendship. He wants it to be an adventure of discovery. He wants to play hide-and-seek with us and give us the joy of finding him in unexpected ways and places.

Pause and reflect

- We all lose things; think back to something you mislaid that was important to you.
- How did you feel as you searched for it?
- How did you feel when you found it?
- Thank your heavenly Father that he always wants to give you the joy of discovering him and his love.

9

Healing Conversations

The word of the Lord came to me...

Jer. 1:4

Are you starting to glimpse the fact that the God you worship as Lord loves to come alongside you? Do you believe that you will hear his voice and that you can talk together? Conversation is an essential part of being human, and while some find it easier than others, we all need to engage in some way, even if it's just discussing the weather with someone at the bus stop. We may converse face-to-face or by phone or text, but the important thing is that we do interact in some way.

- Have you had a conversation today? Who with?
- How would you describe it? Good? Fun? Irritating?
- How did you feel afterwards?

Sometimes I am a bit of a 'name dropper', casually bringing into a conversation that I once had tea with, for example, Ken Dodd or chatted with Bobby Ball . . . It can make us feel significant to say we've met a famous person, especially if we got to chat with them and didn't just gawp from a distance. You've probably had some amazing encounters too? Maybe with the Queen or a great Christian leader? But these encounters, while they may be the highlight of our year, will not usually prove to be life-changing in the way that conversing with God is.

✦ Pause and reflect

- Have you had a conversation with God today?
- What did you say to him?
- What did he say to you?
- How would you describe it? Fun? Enlightening? Puzzling?
- How did you feel afterwards?

A life-changing conversation

The following is taken from one of Marilyn's early songs: 'I Don't Want to Be on My Own' and describes a conversation between someone who is fearful of loneliness as they look into their future, and God's loving response:

> I don't want to be on my own, to be on my own, when I'm old.
> I feel my life is ebbing away and I just don't know where I belong.
>
> *Is it you singing that lonely song?*
> *Do you feel there's nobody you can turn to?*
> *Do you feel there's no one to whom you belong?*
> *O my child, I'm your Father, I'm calling you to come to me . . .*
> *I am the one who gave you your life; I brought you into this world . . .*
>
> Marilyn Baker

Extract taken from the song 'I Don't Want to Be on My Own' by Marilyn Baker. Copyright © 1985 Authentic Publishing.*

Marilyn was inspired to write this after her uncle said, 'I don't want to be on my own when I get old.' Marilyn shared about God's love with him but still felt burdened to put his words and God's answer into a song, realising how many people had the same, deep fear.

I loved the song when I first heard it; not just its haunting words, but its message that we can share in a real way with God and that he will respond. In the song, as the person hears God, their heart is opened and they end by asking Jesus into their life. Truly life-changing!

While that may be great in a song, can we really expect that God will converse with us? Isn't that just taking fantasy a bit too far, like when you have a crush on a celebrity and in your imagination see yourselves enjoying being together? Those imaginings usually stay just that, imaginings, so surely it would be even more so with God?

No.

It's not the same in any degree.

For unlike the celebrity who has never met you and has no idea of your feelings, God not only knows you but actually made you. He is already familiar with all your ways. Listen to this different translation of Psalm 139:1–5:

> Lᴏʀᴅ, you know everything there is to know about me. You perceive every movement of my heart and soul, and you understand my every thought before it even enters my mind. You are so intimately aware of me, Lord. You read my heart like an open book and you know all the words I'm about to speak before I even start a sentence! You know every step I will take before my journey even begins. You've gone into my future to prepare the way, and in kindness you follow behind me to spare me from the harm of my past. With your hand of love upon my life, you impart a blessing to me (ᴛᴘᴛ).

Only the most passionate love would cause God to know you so intimately, and it is out of that love that he calls you to come and spend time with him. He wants to hear what matters to you and also wants to tell you what matters to him, to give you his divine perspective. The following story shows how God can touch our hearts through the most everyday things. This story was shared with me by Claudine.

> I was on the train. During my journey, a father and his very young daughter came to sit in front of me. The father put his little girl on his lap and proceeded to watch something with her on his laptop. He was so utterly engaged with her, smiling, whispering in her ear and kissing her on her head. They got off the train shortly after, but it spoke to me so profoundly of the Father showing how much he loves us, loves me. This earthly father's absolute delight in his daughter was so enthralling

to watch. How much more, our heavenly Father's? This spoke to me so personally because one of my deepest desires is to sit on my heavenly Daddy's lap, nestled against his breast. To feel the warmth of his love and see his affirming smile; to *know* that I'm OK, and not dirty or guilty. There's nothing more I could want.[1]

I felt so moved when I read this. I could identify with her longing to be a child again, loved and safe in her heavenly Father's embrace. What I find amazing is that God knew Claudine's longing, just as it says in that psalm. He wanted to fulfil it so he used the ordinary occurrence of a father and child sitting on the train to minister deeply into her need.

Take a few moments

Your heavenly Father is with you right now. He loves you, and every detail of your life matters to him. Read the above passage from Psalm 139 again and thank him that what you are reading is how he loves *you*.

Using three simple words – 'Father, I feel' – start to share with him. What's on your heart? What are you worrying about? What would you like him to do for you? Listen for his response. He may drop thoughts in your mind, or lead you to a scripture or cause you to notice something that he'll speak to you through. Write down what happens.

God hears and responds

A man with leprosy came and knelt in front of Jesus, begging to be healed. 'If you are willing, you can heal me and make me clean,' he said. Moved with compassion, Jesus reached out and touched him. 'I am willing,' he said. 'Be healed!' Instantly the leprosy disappeared, and the man was healed (Mark 1:40–42 NLT).

This conversation is one of the shortest recorded in the Gospels but is full of wonderful insights.

The leper knew there was no hope for him. Leprosy was an incurable condition causing great suffering not just physically but because of being constantly ostracised by the community. Out of the depths of his physical and emotional pain he came to Jesus. It says he 'begged him on his knees'. You can sense his despair and passionate hope, and yet from his words it is clear that he didn't expect Jesus to respond. His fear had been birthed throughout years of rejection. Have you suffered rejection too? Do you think everyone including God will reject you? That was what he felt. It was out of this prison that the leper begged Jesus for help.

But the wonderful thing is that despite his fears, the leper still chose to come to Jesus to express his longing. This was true prayer, the place where a healing conversation with God starts from. Look at Jesus' response:

> Moved with compassion, Jesus reached out and touched him. 'I am willing' (NLT).

His compassion was tangible and visible – he feels our pain, suffers with us and acts to help us.

He touched the man, thereby becoming ritually unclean himself, but the man's pain was all he cared about. Jesus' touch actually cleansed and healed the man so breaking the old pattern of defilement through touch. Touch can be very healing and sometimes God may just want to give us a loving hug through one of his children.

He reflected the man's words back to him – 'I am willing'. When someone echoes back what you have dared to share, it creates a tremendous sense of being validated. Jesus gave that to the leper and gives it to us too.

'Be clean!' Jesus answered the man's prayer by releasing healing power into his body. God's healing response will always bathe and bless the whole of our lives, including our bodies.

Life-validating conversations

So Jesus validated the leper. What does it mean to be validated?

When you respect and love someone, conversation takes on a whole new depth and can go from laughter to tears in a moment. Often we converse because to sit in silence feels scary. We can spend all our time on safe subjects like the weather or current TV programmes . . . There's nothing wrong with discussing if it's going to be cloudy or breezy tomorrow or who will win *Britain's Got Talent*, but it's hardly the kind of conversation that will change our lives. Validating conversation happens when we are real with someone and they are real with us.

Truly sharing

Read these two fictional conversations and consider which may be the most life-changing.

Conversation 1

Husband:	It was jolly hot in the office today; I had to take my jacket off.
Wife:	It was lovely here. I sat in the park after going shopping.
Husband:	Forecast says it's going to break tomorrow and there'll be rain at last.
Wife:	Oh no! I am doing the washing tomorrow. It can't rain.
Husband:	We need rain, everything's so dry.
Wife:	But why did it have to choose tomorrow? I always do my washing on Wednesdays!
Husband:	Never mind, Mary! Surely you can do it a different day or use the tumble dryer?
Wife:	You don't understand, Dave.
Husband:	I understand all right, you're just too inflexible. Who cares what day you do the silly washing on!

Conversation 2

Husband: It was jolly hot in the office today; I had to take my jacket off.

Wife: It was lovely here. I sat in the park. But how are you, love? You look very tired.

Husband: Well, actually, I'm not great. It was a really stressful day. John was aggressive, saying some horrid things to Margaret and also let loose at Simon. The poor guy was nearly in tears. He's dyslexic and can't help making mistakes, but John made him look an utter fool in front of the whole office.

Wife: Oh, no, that's awful. I know how fond you are of Simon.

Husband: It's not just that I'm fond of Simon, Mary, it's the way John seems to delight in tearing everyone down. I could deck him sometimes, and he never changes. Some folk you know they're just having an off day, but he's horrible all the time.

Wife: Oh, Dave, I never knew you felt like that.

Husband: Well, I'm supposed to be a Christian, I'm not meant to think badly about anyone.

Wife: Don't be daft, Dave, being a Christian doesn't mean you're perfect. Of course you get bad feelings, especially when someone's acting in such a rotten way. Getting angry is a godly reaction as the Lord hates injustice too. You just need to get it off your chest and give it to God to deal with.

Husband: I guess so. I do wonder sometimes if I should leave this job as it gets me so wound up. I know that would be risky . . .

Wife: It's important, though. God doesn't want you to be stuck in something you hate. Let's think, what would you like to do if you did leave?

Did you sense the difference in the depth of communication with these conversations? Both start out focusing on the summer heat, but while the first remained shallow, the second became real communication, a time of sharing and listening, of broaching feelings and expressing half-formed ideas. This happened because the wife looked at her husband properly and sensed that there was something going on that he needed to share. The husband felt valued and thus safe to begin to explore aloud. It's an example of real connection, not just glancing off each other with spiky words.

 Pause to reflect

- Looking back over some of your recent conversations, would you say they have had a safe or a spiky feel to them?
- How do you carry that into your conversations with God?

A growing conversation

The opening quotation from Jeremiah 1:4–7 says:

> The word of the LORD came to me, saying . . .

God initiated this conversation with Jeremiah, who was very young at the time. Here it is quoted more fully, but it would be a good idea to read Jeremiah 1:4–14 yourself:

> The word of the LORD came to me, saying,
>
> 'Before I formed you in the womb I knew you, before you were born I set you apart; I appointed you as a prophet to the nations.'
>
> 'Alas, Sovereign LORD,' I said, 'I do not know how to speak; I am too young.'
>
> But the LORD said to me, 'Do not say, "I am too young." You must go to everyone I send you to and say whatever I command you.' . . .

Jeremiah feels inferior because of his age, but God doesn't want him to invalidate himself for such a reason. God's Word gives him a new identity, and similarly with us, overrides all that we feel disqualifies us.

As the conversation progresses, God teaches Jeremiah to see with spiritual vision rather than just with his natural eyes. Step by step he guides him into his destiny as a prophet. Similar conversations take place countless times throughout both the Old and New Testaments, which is a clear indication that we should expect not just to hear God's voice, but be able to share with him in a real way, hear his response and be changed.

A story

The following story from a dear friend, Susie, shows that God delights in drawing close to us and answering us in such a way that like Jeremiah, we are changed.

Many years ago, Jo and I came back from a wonderful eleven-day cruise celebrating our silver wedding, to discover that my beloved prayer partner had died from a totally unexpected brain haemorrhage and that the funeral had been the previous day. In my devastation, I poured out my anguish to God. He came to me as Father, sheltering me in his strong arms, as Mother, comforting and nurturing; as closest of intimate friends weeping alongside me; and Empathetic Listener who didn't interrupt as I poured out my somewhat irrational thoughts, and then, after a pause, would gently put those thoughts into context. For instance, one day I was inconsolable at the thought that I would never go shopping with her again; until he tenderly pointed out that Merly and I had never been shopping together as that wasn't part of our relationship. He was infinitely patient with me. The depth of his love and care for me at that time was more real than any other love I have ever known, and I look back with great thankfulness.[2]

Pause and reflect

- In this situation, Susie turned to the Lord and shared the turmoil of her grief and discovered he was there for her.
- Looking back on your Christian life, would you say you have ever poured your feelings out to God?
- How did he respond?
- Susie experienced the Spirit gently, even humorously showing her that her train of thought was irrational – have you experienced him giving you a different perspective as you've shared with him? What did he say?
- If you are coping with deep emotions now, why not make some time to pour out your heart to your loving heavenly Father? He longs to hear you and give you his peace.

But how do conversations with God happen?

Think again how God's conversation with Jeremiah began. 'The word of the LORD came to me . . . '

We have been given the mind of Christ (1 Cor. 2:16). We cannot see God, but we can still hear him and tune into his thoughts. A little idea might drop into your mind, the awareness of his goodness on a day when everything is going wrong, a sense of needing to call someone . . . Or he may use something ordinary as a channel for his words, like when Jesus seems to be watching builders at work and sensing God speaking through this about our foundations (see Matt. 7:24–27). The key is that we can hear him but we need to practise our readiness to respond if something draws our attention. Whether it's something visual, a Bible text or his word in our hearts it will have a ring of understanding and truth that pinpoint it as from God.

God understands the things we go through, for he has experienced life in all its joys and sorrows and feels the pain of our infirmities. So like with Susie's experience, his words to us always hit the spot. This is what brings us change as we listen to him.

A story

Marilyn shares how a member of her house group always preached at her rather than engaging her in conversation. One night she crossly told the Lord that she never wanted to sit next to this man again. A thought came that God wanted her to be compassionate towards Stephen. Marilyn replied, 'Why should I? He just sits and lectures me.'

Then a further thought came: 'Stephen recently had a breakdown and can't help talking as he does, but I want you to be praying for him, not knocking him.'

Marilyn was shocked as she'd had no idea about the breakdown. Later she discreetly made enquiries and found it was true. She felt humbled and said sorry to the Lord and asked him to bless Stephen and to change her heart. The following week she was put next to him again but began to quietly pray for him. Stephen started talking, but suddenly Marilyn realised that she was finding his words really interesting and they had a great conversation. Marilyn was full of thankfulness at how the Lord had changed her heart and enabled her to see Stephen from his perspective.

 Pause to reflect

- Have you ever experienced the Lord changing your heart towards someone?
- How did you feel towards the person afterwards?
- We all have challenging people in our lives. If someone is causing you problems, spend a few moments lifting them and your feelings to the Lord. Ask him how he sees them.
- Is there anything he wants you to do, such as pray for them?
- Thank him for this life-changing conversation.

A prophetic word from your heavenly Father

As I was writing, a deep sense came to me of the Father's compassionate understanding of someone's pain. You have been trying to get your head around the concept of him conversing with you, but the more you read, the more pain you feel. It is a pain of lack that you've hardly ever had the experience of being listened to and shared with. The words you did hear crippled rather than nurtured you. You longed to be able to talk to someone, to share your hopes, struggles and joys, but you were ignored and belittled. Now you just don't know how to do it, even if there is someone to listen. You hear yourself as you speak with others and know your own words are awkward, that you often sound dismissive simply because you don't know how to respond. You can tell people are withdrawing from you, nervous of being crushed, and you hate yourself. God wants to give you new hope. He put these words in my heart for you: 'Beloved child, I see your pain and I weep with you. Every tear is precious to me. I know all you have been through and how your natural God-given confidence has been stripped like you might strip wallpaper, leaving the walls scarred and barren. I saw when you came trustingly wanting to show your treasures and share your discoveries, only to be ignored as if you were rubbish. I have seen the words that came like hammers upon your head, punching you down and driving you into the dirt, so weighty was their crushing effect.

'Child, I love you and I long to hear your voice. Your voice and all that you are is so beautiful to me. I am not like those who hurt you. I formed you and have always delighted in you. I want to speak words to you that will heal your heart and set you free from your past wounds. Come just as you are, beloved child. I am not expecting you to have great faith at this stage. But just come in your need for things to be different. I will meet you there and wrap you in my Father's love, and in the stillness of my peace you will start to hear my voice and know that I am the one who always rejoices to affirm you.'

A holy pause

God is with you in all his tenderness and compassion.

Relax in his love.

If you can, thank him for his kiss of affirmation through this word.

Sit quietly just being, and then when you're ready, ask yourself: 'How do I feel?'

Healing conversations

God says through Isaiah how even the strongest of us can struggle and become weary and disillusioned in life if we are only trusting in ourselves, but as we trust in him, there is a wonderful releasing and soaring in our spirits. This is the Father's promise to us all. Isaiah 40:28–31 says:

> He will not grow tired or weary, and his understanding no one can fathom. He gives strength to the weary and increases the power of the weak. Even youths grow tired and weary, and young men stumble and fall; but those who hope in the Lord will renew their strength. They will soar on wings like eagles; they will run and not grow weary, they will walk and not be faint.

I love the phrase 'his understanding no one can fathom'. It makes my heart rejoice knowing how completely I am understood by him. I grew up with such a lack of understanding from those around me that I learned to bury my childlike inquisitiveness and the things that made me uniquely Tracy.

Even after I became a Christian I was still afraid of expressing my preferences to the extent of never choosing a drink, saying instead, 'What are you making?' A crazy response because the choice was usually between tea and coffee, and as I don't drink coffee, there was no contest.

But that passage and others show that God understands us with an understanding no one can fathom. He knows the hiding places we erect in our hearts, but loves us enough not to leave us hidden there.

How does he reveal his understanding? One way can be through other people. I remember when I went on my very first silent retreat, my spiritual director, a young lady called Mags, spent time every day listening to me. Some of the things I shared were trivial, others were terrifyingly deep as I faced my buried memories of abuse and shame. She never said much, she didn't need to because her few words came from a heart that understood not only my pain, but also God's unending compassion. Every time I glanced at her I could see that compassion in her eyes, and the little nods she gave to encourage me that she'd heard and understood. By the end of the retreat I felt turned inside out. I had met with God and knew he loved me, knew he'd gone to that cross for me, knew that I need never hide again because he understood and . . . loved me. I was shaken to the core in the best possible way and this all happened through one of God's children, a woman eleven years younger than me and very different, and yet who was the most life-changing channel of the Father's understanding I have ever met.

The following is a poem which I wrote immediately after that retreat and have dedicated to Mags.

Tenderly, Lovingly

Tenderly, lovingly, you looked within my soul
Saw all the emptiness, shame, and fear
Hidden so long in darkness,
Buried beneath,
All I'd made myself to be
But was not.
Not at the core of my being.

Tenderly, lovingly, you took my hand
To lead me to that place of seeing.
I shrank, must close the door,
But found you, in the gap with me.
Why look back to that dark? I cry
It's beyond the time I knew you.
And in my heart hear your whispered reply
Child, I know, I've always been there.

Tenderly, lovingly, you showed me,
All I'd most dreaded to see.
I'd denied anger, judgement and rage,
Yet, they'd put you on that tree.
And even as I am overwhelmed
Your living forgiveness melts me.
I enter shame, but find you there,
Waiting, arms open to hold me.

Tenderly, lovingly, you reach in
To the very core of me.
You pierce a hole in the centre,
And pour in your life and glory.
And I stand and gaze and I see,
No more just a blank, an awful dark,
But you, in all your beauty.
I ask, I long, I cleave on to you.
Holy sorrow, laughter, peace and joy.
Because in finding you I have found me.[3]

We've looked briefly at a whole range of little pointers to the precious gift God has given us to draw close to him, hear his voice and know that he hears ours. We've thought about his Word coming to our hearts and the way he will use the most ordinary things to speak through. We've thought of how he can use his children to touch or validate us. Let's finish with some final thoughts about the Father's delight in us.

God's delight in us

God started conversing with humankind in the Garden of Eden, when he would come in the cool of the evening and spend time with Adam and Eve. It was to Adam out of all creation that God spoke directly, speaking with words of love and purpose to the man he had just formed. In chapter 2 we see Adam and God working in partnership as God entrusted to him the naming of all his new creations. The Bible can be very brief sometimes, but it doesn't take much imagination to picture the scene. God must have communicated to Adam what he wanted of him, otherwise Adam would have felt very confused when animals of all types started parading in front of him. So God chatted to him, delighting in their togetherness, just as he delights in sharing his kingdom work with us today. I can imagine each animal coming before Adam, either towering over him, fearsome in its size or almost crawling into his hand as he knelt to see it. And Adam expressing his wonder or incredulity, and in turn God his Father, dancing in delight at the appropriateness of each name Adam chooses, cherishing working together with the man he has formed . . .

You may feel that I am just letting my imagination run riot as the Bible doesn't specifically describe it happening that way at all. But if the Bible went into full detail about how things were and God's feelings and the people's feelings, there would be no room to house all that was written. We get glimpses into God's heart from words and phrases scattered through the Old and New Testaments; for example, that he said that all he had made was 'good' or 'very good'. It is clear that there was a great sense of God enjoying making the universe. In Zephaniah 3:17 we can see that God our Father does not suffer from English reserve. He is expressive and uninhibited:

> The LORD your God is with you, the Mighty Warrior who saves. He will take great delight in you; in his love he will no longer rebuke you, but will rejoice over you with singing.

I heard that C.S. Lewis coined a phrase that we all have a 'baptised imagination' once we accept the Lord into our lives. Our imaginations are a wonderful gift that God wove into our minds; the ability to envisage, picture and create the detail. In our spiritual lives, our imaginations can be a means of us encountering God and hearing his voice. So we can take a passage like the one in Zephaniah and use our imagination, asking the Holy Spirit to show us what he wants us to see. It was as I did this that I began to 'see' him dancing with delight over Adam's involvement with creation.

 **Pause to reflect**

- Spend a few moments thinking about your own life.
- Ask God to remind you of something you have achieved.
- How do you feel about that achievement?
- How do you think God feels about it?
- Can you picture him taking great delight and rejoicing over you? What does he do?
- Spend a few moments being celebrated in this way.
- Write down all that came to you.

10

Chosen by the Father

I have called you; I have chosen you
I really love you; I'm always there beside you.
And as you lean on me,
I will give you the resources of Heaven.

Marilyn Baker

Extract taken from the song 'Resources of Heaven' by Marilyn Baker. Copyright ©
1994 Marilyn Baker Music.*

Parental pride

Because God made humanity in his image, the pride and joy we all
feel in our loved ones' achievements must come from him, as he is the
perfect father. Not being a parent, I asked my friends to give me some
snapshots of their feelings about their children. Here are some of their
responses. It's just a tiny glimpse . . .

I cried every time one of my four moved onto something new. I felt
incredibly proud of them, there was a sense of: this is why we've
been investing into them all these years . . . I had such a feeling of
joy: as a Christian parent one of my greatest joys is to see both my
children walking with Jesus as adults. It is my hope that they feel
that I am always there for them . . . Thirty-one years ago I handed my
little family into the Lord's hands. They are all walking with the Lord
now and the three girls have grown into beautiful young women.
One of them will be speaking at a women's group today and they

were encouraging her . . . I was dreading them going away, but would never have stepped in their way, as I was so proud of what they have achieved . . . He went off a bolshie 18-year-old, and graduated a man, I'm so happy . . . The first time I heard my youngest son sing at the senior citizens' Christmas dinner I could hardly hold back the tears . . . It makes me so very happy to see how much they are caring for others . . . I feel like my daughters have gone so much further than I have. I feel that my life has been a stepping-stone for them and I am very proud of them.

 Pause and reflect

- Reading these comments, how do your own children's or loved ones' achievements make you feel?
- Write a few words to express your pride in them.
- Now read this verse from Isaiah 43:4: 'Since you are precious and honoured in my sight, and because I love you . . . ' God honours and loves you. How does that make you feel?
- Write down your response and talk to him about it.

Character not performance

Many of those parents felt particular joy that their children were maturing, making good choices and beginning to look outwards to the needs of others. For Christian parents, there is also celebration when their children develop their own faith. All these things bring our heavenly Father the greatest joy too, for he has chosen us to share in his kingdom work.

If you think of the Bible, it's incredible how frequently God chose those who were weak to fulfil his purposes. For example, Abraham was known as God's friend and took amazing steps of obedience, but also made some dreadful mistakes; Jacob was a cheat, yet was renamed

Israel; Moses was exiled for forty years after committing murder, yet was chosen to be Israel's deliverer and commended for being the most humble man on earth; Rahab was a Canaanite prostitute, yet revered throughout history for saving the Israelite spies; David was the despised youngest son, yet chosen to be king. The Samaritan woman lived a sinful life but became the first evangelist; Gideon was a coward but was called 'Mighty Warrior' and chosen to deliver Israel from the Midianites; Jeremiah lacked confidence because he was so young; Paul was a persecutor and murderer . . .

The thread joining these people together is that although they messed up or felt weak, they still responded to God's loving call. When his love touches our hearts, true faith is born, the faith of intimacy, mutual trust and expectancy.

As Paul teaches us in Hebrews 11:6:

> And without faith it is impossible to please God, because anyone who comes to him must believe that he exists and that he rewards those who earnestly seek him.

Pause and reflect

- Reading the above examples, how does it make you feel to realise that these Bible characters were also weak and fallible?
- Do you hold back from serving God because of believing you are inadequate? Can you tell him you are sorry and want to make yourself wholly available to his call?
- A favourite Bible passage of mine is John 15. Read it slowly and try to sense Jesus' heart for you. Some words are repeated several times, for example, love.
- What is he saying to you?
- Write in your journal any thoughts that come to you and spend time worshipping him.

Called to bear fruit

A strand that keeps running through John 15 is that God has chosen us to bear fruit:

> You did not choose me, but I chose you and appointed you so that you might go and bear fruit – fruit that will last – and so that whatever you ask in my name the Father will give you (John 15:16).

What did Jesus mean? In the context of this chapter, I believe he means more than the character fruits of the Spirit as listed by Paul in Galatians 5:22,23. They are included but he is also pointing to the godly acts that will flow out of such traits. Acts like comforting the mourning, sacrificially helping and praying for those who are held captive to sinful lifestyles, welcoming into our homes those who are lonely or ostracised, and caring for those who are sick . . .

So being God's chosen friend is not only about being loved uncon-ditionally, but also realising that he is saying: 'I have created you to do my works in a way that is unique to you. I trust you and have lifted you up to the same heavenly realms as my Son, and I give you my Spirit that you may hear my voice and pray with my authority.'

A family business

I always love seeing shop signs that say, for example: 'Jones & Sons: Family Butchers since 1950.' It means that a family has devoted itself to that particular enterprise with each successive generation responsible for mak-ing it a viable company. Our royal family are a good example of this. With a family business, the children have their own gifts and strengths to develop the business, and similarly Father God entrusts us to do the works of the kingdom, but gives us unique gifts to work with – gifts that fit our character and our experience. This means that we just need to be ourselves because it's in our uniqueness and even our weakness that he will most use us.

Low self-esteem?

But if we haven't been affirmed much, low self-esteem can be one of the greatest barriers to believing that God trusts and wants to use us. Critical, negative words are so crippling. In a book by Jack Frost called *Experiencing Father's Embrace*, Jack shares how his dad was an angry, driven man who never affirmed him as a boy, instead telling him repeatedly that he wasn't good enough. Jack always strived for approval, which never came. Eventually he became very critical in his own turn, even after becoming a Christian and training for the ministry. He was hurting his family and colleagues by his demeaning manner. It was only when he was overwhelmed by the Father's love that he began to change as his life became rooted on the true foundation of God's unconditional love.

Think!

We can never be loved more than we are right now.

Whether we succeed or fail in human terms, God's love can never change for he always loves us 100 per cent.

Knowing this means we need never strive to earn love and never fear that we will lose it. The only thing that can hold us back is if we fail to believe and live in the truth of his love for us.

Jack Frost was released as he encountered the Lord of love and heard his voice speaking into the wounded areas of his heart. As God's healing flowed, Jack became the loving, pastoral son that God had created him to be. Encountering the Father always has the power to transform us. The following is a prayer conversation with God that I had a few years ago. I was trying to fulfil a writing job but the more I stared at the screen, the blanker I felt. I began to feel depressed and the old lies that I was just a nothing person all came crowding to the surface. I thought I'd try writing down my feelings, and to my amazement I began to hear the Father speaking back to me. This is the conversation:

Staring at a Blank Screen

I am staring at a blank screen wondering what to type;
do I have anything within me to share?
Or am I just a blankness like this screen,
a façade, an outer shell, but nothing of depth in me?
Do I have to await others stronger than I to write their thoughts upon me,
like I write my own upon this screen?
For their opinions to become mine,
and thus come into my own being?
So often this is how I live,
afraid to explore my own thoughts or trust in my own validity,
so I wait for others to give me theirs.
But suddenly I hear the voice of my Father whispering to me:
'Whose hands wove you together in your mother's womb
and lovingly formed your innermost being?
Who painted you with unique colours of joy and love
and touched your DNA with my kiss?
Who celebrated your conception before this world was formed
and danced with delight at your birth?
Could I have created just a nothing, a blank,
a tablet to be written on, but without its own beauty?
Child, I formed you in my image,
dare to believe that I created you in love and I cannot make mistakes.
Live in wonder, joyfully ask and seek and you will find me.
Don't hide behind what others say or think,
but receive their opinions with love and honour
even while rejoicing in living your own uniqueness.
For have I not chosen you to be my bride, my friend, beloved child and heir?
My co-worker whom I trust with my kingdom?
Look within, child, and discover the depths
and dare to live as I've created you to be.'[1]

✦ **Pause and reflect**

- What was your emotional response to my conversation with God?
- Note that he brought the truths of his Word alive in a deeply personal way. This was not just true for me, but for us all.
- Do you struggle with lack of self-esteem?
- Read it again, slowly, and if any phrase catches your attention, stop with that and hold it in your heart.
- Ask the Holy Spirit what he is telling you. How do you need to apply it?

No losers in God's kingdom

Marilyn and I once prayed for a lady called Sara who had grown up longing for her father's approval. I asked the Lord to show me how he saw her, and I had a vision of her running a race, desperately trying to win. Others kept passing her and I could sense her fear and knew she believed that she would only feel accepted if she won. Then I saw the finishing line and Sara was last. All the accolades had been given and only the Lord was waiting for her. The moment he saw her he ran towards her, lifted her onto his shoulders and danced around with her, saying, 'Well done, my beloved one.' 'But I lost!' she muttered, her head down. 'Beloved child,' he said, 'it's never to do with winning; it's to do with getting there, with breaking through the barriers. Any child of mine that perseveres is a winner and in my kingdom there are no losers.'

When I shared this with Sara she was overcome by God's love. She wept for over half an hour as God reached deep into her wounded heart to break the power of the lie that she would never be good enough. He entered her prison of condemnation and released her into joy.

Do you believe you are a loser?

Are you striving to earn God's love?

If that vision speaks to you too and, like Sara, you know you've been desperately striving to earn God's love, then maybe you'd like to pray this prayer with me?

Loving Father, thank you that you sent your precious Son to die for me so that I could be your child and belong to you forever. Thank you that you love me as you love Jesus. Thank you that you always want to encourage me, just because I am your child. Forgive me for trying to earn your love when I already have it 100 per cent. Please help me to live in its truth. In Jesus' name. Amen.

Forgiven

In the Garden of Gethsemane, Jesus needed his friends' support to face the coming horror, but they all fell asleep. Three times they had the opportunity to get their act together, but they slept each time. In Mark and Matthew it says 'their eyes were heavy'; in Luke it says 'they were exhausted from sorrow'. They were grieving, they were afraid, and reacting like we all do when we can't cope. They were burying their heads in the sand and forgetting Jesus' predictions and promises. It was these overwhelming feelings that then led Peter to disown Jesus. Here is what happened in Luke 22:60–62:

> Peter replied, 'Man, I don't know what you're talking about!' Just as he was speaking, the cock crowed. The Lord turned and looked straight at Peter. Then Peter remembered the word the Lord had spoken to him: 'Before the cock crows today, you will disown me three times.' And he went outside and wept bitterly.

Think of those words 'wept bitterly'. If we ever feel condemned about not praying or reading our Bibles enough, imagine Peter's depth of grief at his betrayal of the One he professed to be willing to die for. Regret and remorse are two of the most crippling emotions we can endure. I remember praying for someone whose brother-in-law had killed her sister in a psychotic rage and she was consumed with the belief that it was her fault, a false guilt as she could never have predicted what was going to happen. We can't rationalise our reactions when extreme trauma hits us, but it's important not to allow the pain and regret to shape us long-term with lies of condemnation.

God does not leave us

Jesus never abandons us but draws us out from that place of mourning. In John 21:15–17 Jesus takes Peter aside after cooking breakfast for the disciples and begins an amazing healing conversation. I will quote the end of it here:

> The third time he said to him, 'Simon son of John, do you love me?'
>
> Peter was hurt because Jesus asked him the third time, 'Do you love me?' He said, 'Lord you know all things; you know that I love you.'
>
> Jesus said, 'Feed my sheep.'

Inner healing can be painful because it involves facing up to things we can't bear to remember. So Peter struggled when Jesus kept on asking if he loved him. It actually says that 'Peter was hurt because Jesus asked him *the* third time' as opposed to *a* third time. It was the third time that would carry most emotional pain for Peter, because it was then that the cock crowed and the Lord turned to look at him. Realisation had dawned, and unable to face what he'd done, he'd gone outside and 'wept bitterly'.

What Jesus did in that conversation enabled Peter to be freed from his guilt. If Jesus had only asked him once or twice Peter may still have been berating himself for that defining third denial. God is so wise in how he leads us in healing prayer. When we try to heal ourselves there will always be areas that are buried or left undone. Someone I used to pray for once responded in a disgruntled way when I asked if he needed to forgive. 'You always bring forgiveness into it!' he said. 'I want to move on to other areas.' It was painful for him to remember how people had hurt him and it didn't seem helpful to keep focusing on his need to forgive. But burying his anger would only imprison him in it. When someone has hurt us, it's upsetting to think that all God cares about is letting them off. But that's not what forgiveness is. God knows that we get hooked into that pain and its perpetrator; but our choice to forgive frees us. It's the opposite to letting them off, for they will be in the hands of the perfect judge who will deal with them at the right time; while we will be free to move on.

Forgiveness and inner healing

What Jesus was doing in asking Peter three times if he loved him more than anything else, was completing that work of healing forgiveness. He was undoing what Peter had done and ministering complete restoration. This is the love of our Father who as Psalm 103:3,8–12 says:

> forgives all your sins . . . The LORD is compassionate and gracious, slow to anger, abounding in love . . . he does not treat us as our sins deserve or repay us according to our iniquities. For as high as the heavens are above the earth, so great is his love for those who fear him; as far as the east is from the west, so far has he removed our transgressions from us.

'Abounding' is an old-fashioned word nowadays, but it implies things that are very plentiful, overflowing, or given in large amounts. So this verse means that his love is plentiful, never in danger of running out and never in short supply.

In his great compassion he gives us a visual picture of the fact that he has totally taken away our every sin: 'as far as the east is from the west'.

This is not describing the gap between the east and west of your town or country. He is describing the difference between the east and west of the entire universe. How many millions of light years are there between the planets of our own galaxy, let alone others? To imagine the whole universe is beyond our comprehension, but God inspired David to write this because he wanted us to understand the totality of his forgiveness. There is no way those sins can ever be placed on us again.

A weight of condemnation?

I keep sensing that someone is carrying a heavy weight of condemnation. This is for someone specific and you can't look at people or even pray, as you feel such shame. Like Peter, you have wept many bitter tears and in your memories you keep visiting what you did and it is like a knife tearing you apart. When you hear about God forgiving you, you dare not let yourself believe this can be true for you. So deep is your condemnation that you feel it is right that you be judged and that it would be sacrilege to accept his forgiveness for yourself.

I feel his grief for this weight you are carrying so needlessly. Jesus took the full weight of it onto the cross on your behalf. In his eyes it is already dealt with. I believe he is saying to you now: 'Child, come close, open your eyes and look at me. See what I am carrying for you. Are you shocked to see it is your sin? I know how you have hated yourself ever since. You believe you should be eternally condemned and only you should bear this guilt. You cannot even contemplate that you might be forgiven. Every day you try to take it back from me, despite knowing that you can barely move or even think when you are carrying it alone. Beloved one, come closer. This is no longer your burden to carry. Let me show you; can you see it has got my name on it now, not yours? It is my burden now, not yours. Only I can decide what to do with it and I have already taken it to be destroyed. It is finished. It is gone. You are free, beloved one. You can never have it back. It is gone forever.'

 ## Pause and reflect

- Take a few minutes to be with the Lord.
- Read through the above prophetic word to you again. Dare to believe this is for you personally.
- Do you recognise the heavy weight that the prophecy is referring to? How long have you been carrying it?
- God longs for you to receive his forgiveness. Can you talk to him about what you did? Remember, he is abounding in love and full of compassion.
- Thank Jesus that he chose to carry this sin onto the cross for you. The prophecy urged you to look closely at that weight to see whose

name is on it now. Ask the Holy Spirit to help you see the truth. Tell him that you'd like to receive his forgiveness now.

- Spend time thanking him for his amazing love.

You may like to reflect upon the words of this lovely song of Marilyn's.

Relaxing in the Presence of Jesus

Relaxing in the presence of Jesus
Resting in the shelter of His love
Basking in acceptance and forgiveness
Joined to our Father
Citizens of Heaven above.
Knowing he wants us close beside him
Loved and chosen as his friends
So there's no need to fear,
With gladness we'll draw near
To our Jesus
On whom our joy and hope depends.

Marilyn Baker

'Relaxing in the Presence of Jesus' by Marilyn Baker. Copyright © 1998 Marilyn Baker Music.*

Sons and daughters of God

In my book *Flying Free with God*, I tell the story of how God spoke powerfully to me one day when I was taking Marilyn's guide dog, Pennie, for a walk in the nearby field. It was a cold, murky day and I was hurrying to get round quickly so I could return to my warm home. Suddenly I had an inexplicable feeling I should stop. I looked around, puzzled and in that moment the clouds parted and sunlight poured through, transforming the field into a glittering golden sea. Stillness hung over everything as if creation itself was holding its breath. Even Pennie stood quietly at my side.

I could hardly breathe. I knew that God was there, his presence was overwhelming. It was no accident that the sun had lit up the frost in such a dramatic way just as I happened to be looking. I waited expectantly, knowing something momentous was about to happen.

Seconds ticked by and still the fiery gold lit up the field. It was amazing how it had been transformed into something so glorious. I became aware of a verse – Romans 8:19 – running over and over in my mind:

> For the creation waits in eager expectation for the children of God to be revealed.

This was the key – that the field, when touched by the golden rays of the sun, had been made glorious. In that moment of awareness, God whispered into my heart: 'I have shown you this as a picture of what you and all my sons and daughters truly are in me. You see yourselves as ineffectual, but my glory is within you and upon you. Creation itself and this whole world are waiting for that glory to be revealed. There will be no limit to what I can do when my sons and daughters rise up in their true God-given glory.'

With that, the clouds massed together and the field returned to normal. But as I completed my walk I could not forget what I had seen and its spiritual message. The sense of awe filled me over the next few days. God had come close. He had turned an everyday task into a sacred moment, a meeting with the Eternal. Yet, as profound as this was for me personally, I knew that it was for more than my ears. There were several dynamic elements to that experience, each of which could unlock doors in our lives and enable us to live in a new dimension in our relationship with God:

- God came alongside me in an ordinary place while I was doing an ordinary task.
- God acted and spoke through creation in such a way that I was compelled to stop, look, worship and listen to him.
- It is vital that we know that he has made us to be carriers of his glory, for this will open the created world to God's Spirit and works of love.
- Creation is waiting for this. How long are we going to make it wait?

Our Father calls and equips us

When ministering to Peter, Jesus did something highly significant. Each time Peter answered affirmatively to the question about his love for him, Jesus commissioned Peter to take care of his sheep. In effect, Jesus was saying, 'You are my son and heir. I trust you to work with me in my kingdom.' He was declaring that even Peter, who had failed him so badly, was now a son whom he loved and had chosen.

It was this same message that God was impressing on my heart in the field. We have been chosen, despite our frailty, to be sons, daughters and heirs together with Jesus. As it says in Ephesians 2:4–7:

> But because of his great love for us, God, who is rich in mercy, made us alive with Christ even when we were dead in transgressions – it is by grace you have been saved. And God raised us up with Christ and seated us with him in the heavenly realms in Christ Jesus, in order that in the coming ages he might show the incomparable riches of his grace, expressed in his kindness to us in Christ Jesus.

I find it hard to get my head round what verses like this are really saying, as their meaning seems mind-boggling. Neither can Paul find words to describe how amazing God is, his great love, his kindness, the riches of his grace . . . This is the truth, that you and I, living from that realm of intimacy with God, will have holy authority to make him known.

Personal story

The following is a description of what happened the very first time I went with Marilyn to one of her concerts. I had come to know her the previous summer when I'd been a Christian for about two years and had just finished my degree. I was unsure of my future and was still working through many emotional issues. Although I knew God loved me, I didn't believe he could use me as I felt I was too weak.

So when Marilyn asked me if I could accompany her to some concerts, as her assistant had left, I thought she just wanted me to help her sort out her luggage, clothes and make-up. That was challenging enough, as I'd hardly ever worn make-up, let alone put it on a blind person. But I could cope with that as long as I didn't have to be in public. So I was shocked when Marilyn unexpectedly said: 'Could you share your testimony tonight, Tracy? I've over an hour's programme and it would be lovely if they could hear something about you.'

She had smiled encouragingly, not realising the panic her query had induced in me. How could *I* speak? How could I tell a vast group of people what I'd hardly divulged to one person before? It seemed impossible. But despite my misgivings, something made me say yes and now the concert was beginning. I helped Marilyn to the piano and sat heavily in my own chair. The large congregation stared up at us and I breathed deeply, trying to stop my legs from shaking. For the first time, I was in full view of a big group of people. How could I have done this?

My heart hammering, I gazed out over the sea of faces. Marilyn was singing and as the audience listened, a deep quietness stole over the church and my anxiety eased. I'd not been able to hear music properly for ages, but amazingly I could hear more of Marilyn's songs than I'd expected. Her voice was rich and beautiful, conveying God's love so powerfully that I felt close to tears.

The song ended and I clapped, along with the audience. I was beginning to relax but Marilyn's next words sent me straight back into terror.

'Tracy will now share her testimony with us,' she said, turning round and giving a little nod which was our prearranged sign in case I didn't hear her. The audience stared as I rose on wobbly legs and, with my mind a total blank, walked towards the microphone. All I wanted was to run from the stage and never get on one again.

'Lord, please help me, I can't do this.'

As I opened my mouth, I tangibly felt his presence as if he was standing right next to me. A deep peace filled me and without any plan, I found myself describing the maze of confusion, shame and fear that had made up my childhood; how I'd become a prisoner of self-hatred; my resulting inability to love. I'd hardly admitted these things, even to myself, but now the words came with real fluency. The church was still, faces turned up to me, and people were wiping their eyes. I felt a warm wave of their empathy flowing towards me. They believed me and were listening. I began to make eye contact and suddenly found I was filled with a longing to tell them that God loved them and could truly heal their broken hearts. I shared the miracle of my salvation, the deep healing and transformation that was still unfolding in my life, that he was freeing me to become someone who could reach out with his love instead of hiding away; that this is what he longs to do for each one of us

I finished and glanced at Marilyn. She began to applaud and soon the whole church was clapping. Marilyn continued singing, choosing songs full of joy and celebration. I felt like dancing, there was such a bubble of joy in my heart.

At the end the minister came up, gesturing warmly in our direction as he spoke fervently. Although I couldn't hear him, I guessed that he was making an evangelistic appeal. 'Lord, please may they respond,' I prayed silently. People began to rise to their feet and the hairs on my neck prickled as one by one, they made their way to the front. The band started to play 'Amazing Grace' and tears came to my eyes as I stood and sang. I felt overwhelmed that the Lord was touching these dear people so deeply. We later found out that more than twenty had made commitments or rededicated themselves to the Lord, and many more had responded wanting prayer or blessing.

I little knew then that what I'd considered to be a one-off was the beginning of an amazing ministry partnership that would see me taking steps I would never have dreamt possible. I'd believed I was doomed to failure, but through the power of God's Father love, even my darkest memories would be turned into the ability to touch others' lives with God's love.

We love because he first loved us

In the final chapter we will look at how we might let the Lord's love touch others through us. The truth that 'We love because he first loved us' (1 John 4:19), was what I discovered that night. God took my wounds and then began to use them to touch others with his wonderful compassion, comfort and hope. In God's kingdom, nothing we ever go through in life is wasted.

God said through Isaiah 61:1–4:

> The Spirit of the Sovereign Lord is on me, because the Lord has anointed me to proclaim good news to the poor. He has sent me to bind up the broken-hearted, to proclaim freedom for the captives and release from darkness for the prisoners . . . to comfort all who mourn, and provide for those who grieve in Zion – to bestow on them a crown of beauty instead of ashes, the oil of joy instead of mourning, and a garment of praise instead of a spirit of despair. They will be called oaks of righteousness, a planting of the Lord for the display of his splendour. They will rebuild the ancient ruins and restore the places long devastated . . .

 Pause and reflect

- Spend a few moments thoughtfully re-reading this passage.
- What does it reveal to you of God's Father heart?
- Are there areas of captivity, mourning or despair in your life?
- Ask the Father who promises joy, gladness, comfort and freedom to come and minister in those areas through his Holy Spirit.
- Read the last phrases onwards from 'They will be called . . .'
- Who is 'they' referring to?
- Imagine how God might want to use you to rebuild and restore. Write down any ideas and talk to him about them.
- Thank him for his calling on your life.

11

Channels of His Love

Lord let there be true love in me;
Love that's never dim, love that speaks of him;
Love that never falters, love that never dies;
Love that bears the burden, love that's always wise.
Love that cares for all men, love to banish fear;
Love that will remember God is always near.
Love that's always helpful, love that's always kind;
Love that's always tender bringing peace of mind.
This is what the Spirit tells me that I need,
For the love of Jesus to fill my life indeed.

Marilyn Baker

'Love' by Marilyn Baker. Copyright © 1987 Authentic Publishing.*

The words of the above song were written by a friend of Marilyn's called Maureen. When Marilyn met her, Maureen was living in an old people's home, despite being just 27. She was deaf, virtually blind and epileptic, but she loved the Lord.

One day Maureen said, 'I wish people believed I could do something but no one trusts me.'

'I would love you to do my cleaning for me,' Marilyn said.

Maureen jumped at the idea and came regularly to Marilyn's, travelling alone on two buses. Sometimes she had fits in the middle of cleaning and once in her enthusiasm she cleaned all the non-stick off the oven. She wanted to do her very best for the friend whose loving acceptance meant so much to her. One day she read Marilyn a poem she'd written, saying that she wished it could be set to music. Marilyn was moved, realising the words poignantly expressed God's longing that we be channels of his love. Inspired, she set it to music and then sang it to Maureen, who could just hear it and was thrilled. Maureen died soon afterwards, but even though her life was short and full of struggle, she had a real impact in the way she constantly sought to love and serve others.

Water into wine

In John 2 we read the story of Jesus turning water into wine to save the embarrassment of the young couple who had not ordered enough for their wedding banquet. I love this story as it shows that Jesus enters into every part of our lives – not just the things that we consider spiritual, but everything. Joy and fun are part of God's character and he has created us to blossom through such communal celebration.

On this occasion the wine has run out, so Mary asks her son to save the day. Compared to when Jesus raised Lazarus from the dead or fed the 5,000, a wedding banquet is something very ordinary, yet it is within ordinary life that God wants people to encounter his love. After Mary brought the need to Jesus, this is what happened in John 2:1–11:

> . . . Nearby stood six stone water jars, the kind used by the Jews for ceremonial washing, each holding from eighty to a hundred and twenty litres. Jesus said to the servants, 'Fill the jars with water', so they filled them to the brim.
>
> Then he told them, 'Now draw some out and take it to the master of the banquet.' They did so, and the master of the banquet tasted the water that had been turned into wine. He did not realise where it had come from . . . Then he called the bridegroom aside and said, 'Everyone brings out the choice wine first and then the cheaper wine after the guests have had too much to drink; but you have saved the best till now.'

Pause and reflect

- God is a God of celebration. He is with you at all times, whether you're at a party, a church service, your workplace, home, or a funeral. Do you know him as the friend who rejoices to be with you?
- Your prayers matter to him. One of the key ways we can reach out with the Father's love is through our prayers for one another. Mary told Jesus about the wine crisis. This was like when we pray and bring a need to him. In Matthew 7:7 Jesus teaches us: 'Ask and it will be given to you'. He longs for us to bring both the huge issues and more mundane things, and he promises to hear our prayers.
- Have you brought any needs to Jesus today?
- Jesus asked the servants to fill the jars with water. These jars were normally used for ceremonial washing, so Jesus turning that particular water into wine was very significant. He was saying prophetically, 'You've tried to cleanse yourself from sin with this ceremonial water which has no real power, but I am turning that water into wine, symbolic of my blood shed for you for total forgiveness.'
- Have you drunk of his forgiveness today?
- The water was turned into something with more substance, wine. A wonderful promise that he takes our paltry ability to love, and turns it into something amazing.
- Imagine yourself as that jar of water. See him reaching in to draw some out. Can you see what your 'water' has become now? Thank him for his unlimited resources within you.

Loving because we are loved

As we saw earlier, the following verse sums up the heart of the gospel and of our calling as Christians:

We love because he first loved us (1 John 4:19).

Real love is dynamic. When we receive it, our hearts are freed from judgemental mindsets to honour others. In the world's view, such love is naïve but it is the currency of God's kingdom here on earth. In Acts, when God gave Peter the vision of the unclean animals, Peter's heart was ready because of having already received forgiveness from Jesus. Although Peter struggled to understand the vision, he still listened, and shared the gospel with the Gentile household, an action which bore amazing fruit.

The more we give God's love away, the more it grows. I know this from experience because when people like John and Amanda showed me such acceptance when I was first a Christian, the desire was birthed within me to love others in the same way. God's love transformed my emptiness into a passion for people to know they belong. Similarly, Marilyn's loving trust enabled Maureen to reach out, despite her limitations. If we all had the vision to love with his love, think of the impact on our broken world.

 ## Pause and reflect

- Thinking of that verse: 'We love because he first loved us', ask the Holy Spirit to remind you of a time when you experienced God's acceptance through someone reaching out to you.
- How did it make you feel?
- Would you say that you accept others as he accepts them?
- What fruit have you seen in your own life and in those you're reaching out to?

Living as a son – a story of healing and release

Once, Marilyn and I prayed with a man who was a successful company director. He'd become a Christian and was challenged by his elders to live his life for God instead of wealth and success. But he didn't know how to do that, as all he knew was business. As we prayed, God spoke in my heart, 'Tell him my plan is for him to truly become my son.' I felt a bit puzzled, but the Lord just kept saying 'I love him as my son. Tell him my plan for him is that he be my son.'

When I shared this, John looked confused. 'But that's just what I am, not what I do,' he said.

'Do you really know what it means, though?' I asked. 'God is saying he loves you as his son and wants you to truly know that. Have you experienced his Father love?'

To my surprise John turned his face away and was obviously struggling with emotion. 'I was a failure as far as my father was concerned,' he said. 'He was always disappointed in me and I could never live up to his expectations. I liked art but that was contemptible to him. He was a hard-headed businessman and I thought he would only ever approve of me if I became a businessman too. So I threw away all my sketches and took a business degree and have succeeded. But' – he swallowed – 'he died of a heart attack last year. I had just won an award for my company but he never acknowledged it. He died still seeing me as a failure, even though I'd given everything, even the path I followed in life, in the hope of earning just one word of approval.' John buried his face in his hands. 'If God is also saying I must reach an invisible summit before I'll be accepted as his son, I just can't do it, I am empty, I have no joy, I am exhausted.'

'John,' Marilyn said softly. 'Father God is saying the very opposite. He loves you *now* as his son. You are already there in the centre of his approval. He rejoices over you and says how proud he is of you. He knows your heartbreak and wants to give you the joy of knowing you are beloved. This is his plan for you. It's what you are already but he wants you to experience it.'

We began to pray, asking the wonderful Comforter to come into John's heart in a new way and release him from the lie that he was a failure. We prayed for Father God to embrace him and enable John to know he was wanted, loved and affirmed. The Spirit touched him in a beautiful way and he tangibly relaxed and was smiling by the end.

Months later we had a message to say how life-changing that time had been, and he was now learning how to live as God's beloved son. Later he wrote again to say that God was leading him to use his business skills to set up many schemes abroad, including helping poor children discover the joy of creativity. He said this had all come out of knowing that he was loved as a son.

 Pause and reflect

- Thinking of what happened in John's life, what was the difference between what he was doing before and what he was doing after the prayer?
- Does his story gel with you at all?
- When God said, 'my plan is that you be my son', how does that speak to you?
- Spend some time with your Father offering him all your gifts, strengths, weaknesses and life experiences. As his beloved son or daughter, how does he want to use you to reach out to others with his love?

Nitty-gritty love

Jesus lived out loving in action – touching lepers, cuddling children, reassuring the thief, lovingly ministering to prostitutes. Story after story of love made real in real people's lives.

Paul describes such love movingly in 1 Corinthians 13:4–8:

> Love is patient, love is kind. It does not envy, it does not boast, it is not proud. It does not dishonour others, it is not self-seeking, it is not easily angered, it keeps no record of wrongs. Love does not delight in evil but

rejoices with the truth. It always protects, always trusts, always hopes, always perseveres. Love never fails.

These words are the nitty-gritty of love. We may experience God's love saturating us, or have an overwhelming encounter with the Holy Spirit. Such experiences are wonderful but the reality is that God loves us all the time, whether we can feel it or not. We know he loves us through his patience in constantly forgiving us even though we mess up so often; through him rejoicing over us and persevering in bringing to life the gifts he has woven into our lives; through him answering our prayers and trusting us to do his works. If we have eyes to see, we will recognise the evidence of his love every day through the ordinary things and people around us.

Jesus broke down the fences

In all social spheres, people bond best with those who think or act in similar ways. It's great when those groups are inclusive, but all too often such groups become cliques characterised by exclusiveness. From street gangs to high-flying business elites, only those who 'fit' can join. This age-old pattern is lived out in every culture. But Jesus was different. Jesus would reach out to people who in the eyes of the crowd were not fit even to be noticed, let alone touched. His closest friends were part of this judge and exclude culture, but Jesus was always ready to honour someone that everyone else rejected.

It's not that sin didn't matter. Jesus went to the cross and suffered the most horrific death and separation from his Father in order to carry the weight of our sins. But his focus was different. He saw each person as worthy of being loved, and that meant choosing to focus on what that person could become, not on their failures.

Every time he healed someone or told a parable, he wanted both those being ministered to and those watching, to be changed. It says in Mark 3:5, when he was healing a man with a shrivelled arm that 'He looked around at them in anger . . . deeply distressed at their stubborn hearts . . .' I find those words very convicting. How often do I bring him deep distress through being judgemental about someone? We need to let go of our judgements and fixed views and allow our hearts to become soft and full of his compassion.

 Pause and reflect

- Will we let our hearts be responsive to his love?
- Is our focus on a person's problem areas that make him difficult to love, or is it on the Lord who created him in his image?
- Will we be true sons and daughters of the King to include all in our circle, not just those who we feel safe with?

Faith in action

The three books of John make it very clear that if we say we know God, our faith has to be shown in our actions. We cannot be closet Christians, and if we are, it means that God's love has not been made real in our hearts. John taught us in 1 John 3:16–18:

> This is how we know what love is: Jesus Christ laid down his life for us. And we ought to lay down our lives for our brothers and sisters. If anyone has material possessions and sees a brother or sister in need but has no pity on them, how can the love of God be in that person? Dear children, let us not love with words or speech but with actions and in truth.

It was frequently said about Jesus that he was 'moved with compassion' (e.g. Matt. 9:36 TPT). In biblical times that would mean moved to the depths of his guts because the stomach or the liver was thought to be the seat of emotion. Jesus wept at Lazarus' tomb, weeping out of empathy for those he loved who had lost their beloved brother. He was not ashamed to show his emotions even though he would soon bring Lazarus back from the dead.

- What does this kind of love say to you?
- Have you ever experienced someone weeping with you when you shared your broken heart? How did that make you feel?
- Have you ever wept with someone else in that way?

Making a choice

We need to make the choice to love, because love is as much to do with our minds and wills as with our emotions. In 2 Samuel 9:1,7,8 there is a telling story. David has finally become king after years of persecution from Saul. At last he is in an exciting season. Such moments can be heady, but David doesn't forget those around him:

> David asked, 'Is there anyone still left of the house of Saul to whom I can show kindness for Jonathan's sake?'

The answer was that Jonathan had a disabled son, Mephibosheth, who was lame in both feet. When David had him called, Mephibosheth was obviously afraid, but David honoured him:

> 'Don't be afraid,' David said to him, 'for I will surely show you kindness for the sake of your father Jonathan. I will restore to you all the land that belonged to your grandfather Saul, and you will always eat at my table.'

> Mephibosheth bowed down and said, 'What is your servant, that you should notice a dead dog like me?'

'Dead dog' wasn't just a melodramatic negative way of thinking about himself, it was literal too. He was a member of Saul's vanquished family, the family that had caused David so much pain. It would have been natural in that culture for the whole family to be destroyed or at least spurned. Mephibosheth was also disabled and only fit to beg. He was helpless, but suddenly the king was offering him his own land and an ongoing invitation to eat at the king's table, the highest honour that could be given. This is also a wonderful prophetic picture of how the Lord raises us up and seats us with him and welcomes us to his heavenly banquet.

David made a choice to show kindness to someone that most would have just dismissed. The result was that Mephibosheth became like a prince instead of a pauper, again a prophetic picture of what God has done for us.

 ## Pause and reflect

- As you think of these two aspects of genuine love, that it is both a compassionate, heart response, and a choice to be acted upon, ask the Lord to show you when someone has responded compassionately to your own needs or chosen to serve you in some way.
- Now ask him to help you to respond compassionately to any needs in the people around you. Is there anything he wants you to do for them?
- If you become aware of any negative reactions holding you back, remember he knows and loves you. Ask him to deal with those issues so that you can be free to love as he loves.

A modern story of life transforming love

In recent years I have been deeply challenged by the ministries of Heidi and Rolland Baker who head up Iris Global, a humanitarian Christian ministry to the world's poorest people. One place where they have had great impact is Mozambique where God led them to rescue and feed countless numbers of children who were literally living on garbage heaps, abandoned and traumatised by war and violence. Heidi became 'Mama' to these children and her simple yet

dynamic faith has seen the Lord providing miraculously and transforming lives that have been devastated. Do read their amazing
book *Always Enough*, but one particular story which I will share is
when they found a little girl of about 10. In Heidi's words, 'her belly
was big and bloated. Flies attracted to fluid crawled around her in-
fected eyes. Open, running sores twisted her face . . . Lice and scabies
covered her.' Beatrice had no family other than an alcoholic father
who had abandoned her. She'd been raped repeatedly and was
dying. Heidi says:

> When I saw her my heart broke. I felt an overwhelming love for this
> wounded child. I saw Jesus in her eyes when I looked at her. I held
> her close and brought her home . . . I got lice and scabies too, but that
> didn't matter. More important was holding Beatrice close and letting
> her know she was valued and loved. She so desperately needed to be
> touched, cherished and hugged.

The whole family became involved in loving Beatrice, even their
10-year-old daughter who gave her best dress. Heidi says: 'Beatrice
treasured that dress and wore it until it was threadbare.'

Although their doctors thought Beatrice would die, God healed her
and in Heidi's words: 'Beatrice responded to the Lord instantly . . . she was
so delighted to know that Jesus loved her, that we loved her and that she
wouldn't be raped any more . . . '

Beautiful as that was, even more happened, for Beatrice then began
to reach out to another little girl of 5, Constancia, who had also been
abandoned. Heidi says 'She was so traumatized that she couldn't
speak . . . She was filled with inexpressible grief.'

Beatrice understood Constancia's deep pain and reached out,
spending lots of time with her. One day, Constancia indicated that she
wanted to be baptised. In Heidi's words:

> When she came up out of the water she smiled for the first time . . .
> and suddenly began speaking . . . Later she told us that she had seen
> her parents shot and their heads cut off. Until then we had no idea

what horror had so frozen her spirit. But Jesus came to her in that baptismal water and turned her mourning into joy. Both Beatrice and Constancia want to be missionaries and lay their lives down for him.[1]

What was happening?

This story is deeply moving because it shows the power of God's love to heal broken hearts. I long to love like this, but fears and inadequacy easily hold me back. But rather than my inadequacy, I need to focus on God's great love. Beatrice teaches us, for she internalised the love she was shown and then reached out with compassion to Constancia. Out of her suffering was born deep empathy. It grieves me to think how terribly these children suffered, but through God's love flowing through Heidi, great power has been released to transform others' lives. How many will be impacted as these young girls give away the love they have received?

Can we love like this?

What also challenges me is how Heidi and her family saw these two broken children. Beatrice was infested with parasites, but Heidi hugged her and their daughter gave her best dress. What did they see in Beatrice that empowered them to love her like this? The key is in Heidi's words: 'I saw Jesus in her eyes when I looked at her.' Rather than seeing a filthy, dying child, they saw Jesus. Rather than feeling revulsion and fear, they felt an overflow of the Father's love. They were living out Jesus' parable of the sheep and the goats, Matthew 25:31–40:

> … All the nations will be gathered before him, and he will separate the people … as a shepherd separates the sheep from the goats. He will put the sheep on his right and the goats on his left.

Then the King will say to those on his right, 'Come, you who are blessed by my Father; take your inheritance, the kingdom prepared for you since the creation of the world. For I was hungry and you gave me something to eat, I was thirsty and you gave me something to drink, I was a stranger and you invited me in, I needed clothes and you clothed me, I was ill and you looked after me, I was in prison and you came to visit me.'

Then the righteous will answer him, 'Lord, when did we . . . ?'

The King will reply, 'Truly I tell you, whatever you did for one of the least of these brothers and sisters of mine, you did for me.'

 Pause and reflect

- Have you ever had the sense that in serving someone in need you are literally serving Jesus? How has that impacted you?
- Heidi's love for Beatrice had the immediate impact of bringing her to Jesus. Have people opened up to God's love as a result of your care? Thank the Lord for them.
- Thinking of the parable, what do these areas of need represent in the lives of people around you? We can be symbolically naked or in prison, i.e. vulnerable or ashamed because of hurt or sin in our lives. Similarly we can be symbolically hungry, i.e. for love, as well as for food . . .
- Have you ever experienced people reaching out to you when you were in need? What impact did it have on you?
- Are you aware of times when you could have reached out to someone but didn't? What stopped you?
- Thinking of Jesus' words in verse 45, 'whatever you did not do for one of the least of these, you did not do for me', do you want to say anything to him?
- Remember, there is no condemnation; he loves you and longs to help you to love without fear. As John teaches us in 1 John 4:18:

There is no fear in love. But perfect love drives out fear . . . The one who fears is not made perfect in love.

- Ask him to wash away all fear and free you from all restrictions to you loving as he loves. Thank him for giving you his perfect love every day.

The greatest commandment

We cannot give away what we haven't got, and it is receiving his love that births our ability to love, not us striving to obey 'ought to's. Sometimes it can seem so spiritual to say, 'I know God loves (or forgives) me, but I can't forgive myself.' We feel we are being humble, but what we are really doing is despising all that Jesus endured on the cross for us. This is why Jesus said when questioned about the greatest commandment:

> 'Love the Lord your God with all your heart and with all your soul and with all your mind.' This is the first and greatest commandment. And the second is like it: '*Love your neighbour as yourself*' (Matt. 22:37–39, emphasis mine).

Are you kind to yourself?

One of the attributes of God's love is kindness, which is a beautiful, everyday way of loving. We've all been uplifted by kind people – someone making you a cuppa, someone giving up their seat on the bus, or sending you a card when you're unwell; holding the door open, or on a deeper level, stopping people's criticisms with a kind word.

Receiving an act of kindness can make our day and many of us excel at giving it. But how often do you extend such kindness to yourself? For example, giving yourself time to relax when you're tired; treating yourself to something nice; reading a book or watching a good film instead of desperately trying to get all the chores done? Allowing someone to help you in some way?

When I first met Marilyn and her blind housemate, Penny, they knew I was deaf but I didn't tell them about my balance and sight problems because I felt embarrassed. They were blind so I was there to help them. I couldn't avoid being upfront about my deafness, as it was obvious, but to me, the most important thing was helping them.

One day Penny asked me to take Marilyn's tea to her, but when I tried, the mug was too full. 'I'm so sorry, Pen,' I muttered, feeling ashamed. 'I can't carry it so full with my bad balance.'

Penny looked dumbstruck for a moment and then smiled and said, 'Oh, no worries, Trace.' She easily took the mug to Marilyn and then, giving me a big hug, said, 'Thanks for letting us know things can be difficult for you, Trace, that really helps us.'

Later, I realised that both Marilyn and Penny had been struggling with my determination to be the one who had to help them. Sometimes it had made them feel rather small! But as soon as I admitted that I too needed help, a barrier was broken and we were able to enter the give-and-take of true friendship. Penny has gone to be with the Lord now, but Marilyn and I are still the closest of friends after thirty-two years. My sight and hearing are now much worse, and although I do still help Marilyn with many things, she daily serves me in amazing ways too, by typing out conversations and other important things, so that I can always be part of what's going on. It's wonderful to both be able to give and receive.

 Pause and reflect

- I helped Marilyn and Penny the most, not with the things I did for them, but by admitting I needed their help too.
- How easy do you find it to admit you need help?
- Ask your heavenly Father to show you any changes you may need to make in how you view yourself so you can truly love others as you love yourself.

Who does God want us to love?

Not many of us will be faced with the kind of situations that Heidi and Rolland contend with, but we are all called to love. Heidi described loving very simply as 'just love the one in front of you.'[2] I love that idea! Even those without family or close friends still have people passing through their lives. If God truly watches over all our comings and goings as it says in Psalm 121, then nothing ever happens by chance. The people that you work with or who you meet behind the till or in the doctor's surgery are all loved and known by God. He wants to be Father to them just as he loves to be Father to you. 'Just love the one in front of you.' How can we do that?

Stepping through intimidation

I love the story of Ananias in Acts 9:10–18. The murderer Saul has been blinded by God's power and is now in Damascus where still blind, he remains for three days praying and fasting. Then the Lord asks Ananias to minister to Saul . . .

The Lord called . . . 'Ananias!'

'Yes, Lord,' he answered.

The Lord told him, 'Go to the house of Judas on Straight Street and ask for a man from Tarsus named Saul, for he is praying. In a vision he has seen a man named Ananias come and place his hands on him to restore his sight.'

'Lord,' Ananias answered, 'I have heard many reports about this man and all the harm he has done to your holy people in Jerusalem. And he has come here with authority from the chief priests to arrest all who call on your name.'

But the Lord said to Ananias, 'Go! This man is my chosen instrument to proclaim my name to the Gentiles and their kings and to the people of Israel. I will show him how much he must suffer for my name.'

Then Ananias went to the house and entered it. Placing his hands on Saul, he said, 'Brother Saul, the Lord – Jesus, who appeared to you on the road as you were coming here – has sent me so that you may see again and be filled with the Holy Spirit.'

Immediately . . . he could see again . . . He got up and was baptised . . .

Ananias was so like us, he could obviously hear the Lord yet suffered the same fears that we do. When the Lord first asked him to go to Saul, all Ananias could think of were the bad reports. If we feel intimidated when we hear a certain person is difficult, how much more natural was Ananias's fearful reaction? Saul was a powerful Pharisee and could easily have Ananias killed.

But when Ananias tells God these 'facts' about Saul, God's response was to show him a different perspective. He had chosen Saul to fulfil a mighty calling and he wanted Ananias to show his love and welcome Saul into the family of believers.

God's love is powerful to free us from fear, and it is clear that by the time Ananias reaches Saul's accommodation, his heart has melted and his attitude changed. He touches Saul with a warm gesture of kindness and then calls him 'Brother'. How beautiful. Ananias opened his heart to God's love, welcoming this violent persecutor into the Christian family. We are still feeling the impact today.

A personal example

On a different but still powerful level, I was once out for a meal with my sister and her friends. I get intimidated socially because of not being able to hear, and on this occasion, I was really struggling. Apart from my sister, I didn't know anyone, and they were all very sociable. The food was delicious but just as I had feared, I couldn't join in.

I felt miserable and was staring down to avoid eye contact, when a clear thought came.

'Why are you staring at your plate? Surely there are more interesting things to look at?'

'Where else am I supposed to look?' I muttered.

'You could try smiling, surely that would be better than gazing at cold curry?'

'But Lord,' I said, recognising this was him, 'they are all so "together". They don't have problems. I just don't fit in.'

'Child,' he said, 'only you of all these ladies is the daughter of the King! How can you say they have everything when you have the very King of this universe sitting with you? How can you possibly know they don't have problems? I want to bless these ladies through your prayers.'

I was astonished and did start to look at those around me, and he began dropping tiny glimpses of their needs into my heart: that one feels lonely; this one fears being made redundant; that one is worried for her youngest child . . .

As I prayed quietly, a deep joy filled my heart. I knew I was on a love mission with the King of kings, secretly blessing each person with his love. The self-pity dissolved as I continued. I even started chipping in. I still didn't know if my stories fitted with the conversations, but it no longer mattered. I knew the Lord's love was touching them all through my prayers. At the end of the evening I still hadn't heard a word, but I left with my head held high. I'd arrived as Miss Inferior. I left as a princess, the daughter of the King.

 Pause and reflect

- In our different ways, both Ananias and I were challenged to step out of our negative perspectives and act with God's love instead of judgement.
- Have you ever sensed the Lord similarly challenging you?
- How did you respond?
- The Lord asked Ananias to visit Saul and pray for him, and he asked me to intercede for the ladies. Have you experienced him asking you to show his love in these particular ways? What effect did it have on the person and on you too? What other ways does he use you?
- Ask the Holy Spirit to anoint you as a channel of his love.

What makes us feel loved?

What makes one person feel loved will be different to another. The media focuses on physical touch, but that is just one of many ways of showing love. Dr Gary Chapman, in his books on the five love languages, specifies five love patterns which although he is teaching from the perspective of romantic love, can equally apply to other relationships. The five areas are: physical touch, acts of service, quality time, words of affirmation and gifts. We need love through all these ways, but there is a primary love-shaped hole that when it is filled, makes us know that we are truly loved.

My primary love language is words of affirmation, maybe because I had so little of it as a child. Whenever someone affirms or even just listens to me in a way that conveys respect, I feel the joy of being loved and I rise up tall within myself. Many people really bless me with kind acts such as typing conversations onto my iPad at social occasions or at church so that I can know what is being said. That gives me great joy but doesn't make me feel loved like affirmation does.

But Marilyn's primary love language is acts of service, so if I make her a hot-water bottle or if a friend sews up a hole for her, Marilyn feels so loved.

I enjoy giving and receiving hugs, but for some a hug or kind touch is all they need. Maybe the fact that Jesus deliberately touched some who came to him for healing, was a sign he knew that this would give them a deep sense of being loved.

I love gifts, especially books or chocolate! But although such gifts do bless me, I would feel just as loved if no one ever gave me a gift again. Paul, however, often rejoiced in people's gifts, so that may have been his love language?

We know people who, when they just spend time with us, come alive and obviously feel loved. Quality time is their love language and strengthens them to cope with life. Peter was someone to whom Jesus gave quality time on several occasions, taking him aside to give him personal attention.

So Jesus reacted differently to different people. One he would spend time with, another he would affirm, another give a gift to, or touch, yet another, serve with an act of kindness. We too can become aware of that primary way of loving as we watch people for clues and listen to the Holy Spirit's counsel. I find this really exciting, to be part of his love mission, effectively giving away the love he constantly gives me.

Pause and reflect

- As you've read about the love languages, what makes you feel particularly loved? Ask the Father to show you how he fills that primary love need in your life.
- Now think about others in your life. Ask him how he wants to use you to reach their primary love needs. Jot down any ideas that come to you.
- Maybe you'd like to pray this prayer with me?

Thank you, Father, that you love me unconditionally, and that because of Jesus I am now your beloved child. Thank you that I am held forever in your embrace. Thank you that you have chosen me to be a channel of your love. Please help me to show everyone in my life your Father heart, just as you have shown me. Anoint me with your love and power. In Jesus' name. Amen.

Conclusion

Your heavenly Father loves you and is committed to you. I hope that as you've read through this book you've begun to experience his love for yourself. Whatever you've been through and whatever regrets you carry, his love is so much bigger and his joy and pride in you so real.

Writing this has been quite a roller coaster for me, as it has brought up so many memories, but looking back I can see how repeatedly he has demonstrated his Father love to me and I am full of thankfulness that he has made me his child. It's my prayer that through some aspect of this book, whether a teaching point, a personal story, a prophecy, poem or reflection that your heart has also been opened to the Father's deep affection for you and that you will keep on growing in his love. May it be the start of a life-long adventure, living closely with the God who loves you so much and discovering the joy of giving that love away to those around you.

Bibliography

I have been inspired by many wonderful teaching and testimony books bringing alive God's love and his power to transform us. The following is a short list. I have quoted from some of these in this book and others have been personal sources of blessing and growth. It would be impossible to list all of them, but maybe this will inspire you to search for your own books that will help you grow in his love.

Adams, Julian, *The Kiss of the Father: Rediscovering a Personal Relationship with the Holy Spirit* (Kent: River Publishing & Media, 2015).

Baker, Heidi and Rolland, *Always Enough* (Ada, MI: Chosen Books, 2012 – ebook).

Blackie, Margaret, *Rooted in Love* (Western Cape, South Africa: New Voices Publishing, 2013).

Chambers, Oswald, *The Love of God* (Crewe: Oswald Chambers Publ. Assoc., 1938).

Chapman, Gary, *The 5 Love Languages* series of books published by Northfield Publishing (Chicago, IL).

Frost, Jack, *Experiencing Father's Embrace* (Shippensburg, PA: Destiny Image Publishers Inc., 2002).

Manning, Brennan, *Abba's Child: The Cry of the Heart for Intimate Belonging* (Colorado Springs, CO: NavPress, 1994).

Manning, Brennan, *The Furious Longing of God* (Colorado Springs, CO: David C. Cook, 2009).

Owen, Emily, *Still Emily: Seeing Rainbows in the Silence* (Milton Keynes: Malcolm Down Publishing, 2016).

Rees Larcombe, Jennifer, All her books!

Simmons, Brian, *I Hear His Whisper* (Savage, MN: Broadstreet Publishing Group, 2015).

Simmons, Brian, *Letters from Heaven by the Apostle Paul* (The Passion Translation) (Savage, MN: Broadstreet Publishing, 2014).

Simmons, Brian, *Psalms: Poetry on Fire* (The Passion Translation) (Savage, MN: Broadstreet Publishing Group, 2014).

Simmons, Brian, *Song of Songs: Divine Romance* (The Passion Translation) (Savage, MN: Broadstreet Publishing, 2014).

Stibbe, Mark, *My Father's Tears: The Cross and the Father's Love* (London: SPCK, 2014).

Stibbe, Mark, *The Father You've Been Waiting For* (Milton Keynes: Authentic Media, 2006).

Silvester, Margaret, *Stepping Stones to the Father Heart of God* (Lancaster: Sovereign World Ltd., 2012).

Williamson, Tracy, *Flying Free with God* (Bognor Regis: New Wine Press, 2008).

Notes

1. What is the Father's Kiss?

[1] © 2009 Brennan Manning. *The Furious Longing of God* is published by David C Cook. All rights reserved. Publisher permission required to reproduce.

3. Struggling with the Concept

[1] Mark Stibbe, *My Father's Tears: The Cross and the Father's Love* (London: SPCK, 2014).

4. Laying the Foundations

[1] 'Creator Without Apology', Tracy Williamson, composed 2006.
[2] With thanks to Fiona M.
[3] 'Mother and Child', Tracy Williamson, composed 2013.

5. You Matter to Him

[1] With thanks to Sharon.

6. Noticing the Father's Presence

[1] With thanks to Wendy Hart.
[2] Tracy Williamson, *Flying Free with God* (Bognor Regis: New Wine Press, 2008).

7. Getting to Know Your Father

[1] Part quoted and part paraphrased from Tracy Williamson, *Flying Free with God* (Bognor Regis: New Wine Press, 2008).

8. Revelation of the Father's Love

[1] With thanks to Lilian Wild.

9. Healing Conversations

[1] With thanks to Claudine.
[2] With thanks to Susie Marriott.
[3] 'Tenderly, Lovingly', dedicated to Mags Blackie, composed 2004.

10. Chosen by the Father

[1] 'Staring at a Blank Screen', Tracy Williamson, composed 2016.

11. Channels of His Love

[1] Heidi and Rolland Baker, *Always Enough* (Grand Rapids: Chosen Books, 2012).
[2] From Heidi Baker's teaching at a conference, The River Centre, Tonbridge, around 2008 (author unsure of date).